CARLOS ACOSTA

MARGARET WILLIS' interest in ballet stems from a five-year stay in the former Soviet Union (1976–81) where she studied classical ballet and began writing on dance. Visiting Cuba in 1990, she first saw Carlos Acosta and has continued to follow his stellar career. She was a member of London City Ballet from 1990–93, performing principal character roles, is the author of *The Russian Ballet on Tour* and has contributed several articles for the *International Dictionary of Ballet*. She writes regularly for the *Dancing Times*, *Dance Magazine* and other international publications. In 1986, she was the researcher for a BBC TV documentary on the Bolshoi Ballet.

CARLOS ACOSTA
The Reluctant Dancer

MARGARET WILLIS

Arcadia Books Ltd
15–16 Nassau Street
London W1W 7AB

www.arcadiabooks.com

First published by BlackAmber Inspirations,
an imprint of Arcadia Books 2010

Series Editor: Rosemarie Hudson
Copyright Margaret Willis © 2010

A catalogue record for this book is available from the British Library.

ISBN 978-1-906413-71-2

Typeset in Minion by MacGuru Ltd
Printed and bound in the United Kingdom by CPI Cox & Wyman, Reading, RG1 8EX

Arcadia Books gratefully acknowledges the financial support of Arts Council England.

Arcadia Books supports PEN, the fellowship of writers who work together to promote literature and its understanding. English PEN upholds writers' freedoms in Britain and around the world, challenging political and cultural limits on free expression.
To find out more, visit *www.englishpen.org* or contact
English PEN, 6–8 Amwell Street, London EC1R 1UQ

Arcadia Books distributors are as follows:

in the UK and elsewhere in Europe:
Turnaround Publishers Services
Unit 3, Olympia Trading Estate
Coburg Road
London N22 6TZ

in the USA and Canada:
Dufour Editions
PO Box 7
Chester Springs
PA, 19425

in Australia:
The Scribo Group Pty Ltd
18 Rodborough Road
Frenchs Forest 2086

in New Zealand:
Addenda
Box 78224
Grey Lynn
Auckland

in South Africa:
Jacana Media (Pty) Ltd
PO Box 291784
Melville 2109
Johannesburg

Arcadia Books is the *Sunday Times* Small Publisher of the Year

If God gives you a gift, it doesn't matter what colour you are. That gift is within you, and nothing, nothing need stop it. You must always follow your dream.

Carlos Acosta

Your destiny is in your hands – you cannot forget that. That's what we have to teach all of our children. It also means pushing our children to set their sights a little bit higher.

Barack Obama

Dancers are the athletes of God.

Albert Einstein

Contents

Introduction

SILENCE DESCENDS ON THE AUDITORIUM as the conductor raises his baton and the music begins. The
curtains draw back to reveal a brilliantly lit stage,
the audience anticipates. Suddenly from the wings,
the Cuban 'missile' strikes, shooting across the open
space in awe-inspiring, powerful airborne leaps
which defy gravity and human force, while his fast
spinning turns seem to bore holes in the flooring.
Carlos Acosta, the once reluctant dancer, has arrived.
The spine-tickling thrill felt throughout the auditorium is evident as breaths are sucked in with excited
admiration, not just because of the new tricks the
muscular dancer has perfected, but because everything he does stems from a pure classical ballet technique – and from the heart.

To most people, ballet is a mysterious art. Unlike
theatre, film, music and opera, little is known of it outside its hallowed studios in the real world. A predicted
description of ballet from the man-on-the-street

would be that the women dance on their tippy-toes while the men wear tights. Unlike the pop star world, ballet dancers and company seasons come and go unnoticed with little fanfare – only their aficionados are switched into the art's remarkable powers to thrill.

Just occasionally do ballet exponents become household names – and for obvious reasons. Rudolf Nureyev, the Russian Tatar, was the first in recent years to hit the world's headlines when, in 1961, he made his dramatic leap for freedom to the West from the Kirov Ballet bringing with him a new style of powerful, macho male dancing. Then thirteen years later came Mikhail Baryshnikov, also an escapee from the stifling Soviet system. With his boyish charm and softer bravura technique, he presented a different brand of male dancing to the world's stages, and later reached a wider audience with appearances in films and television series.

And then there is Carlos Acosta, born in Cuba, with a background of deprivation, physical punishment and reluctance, who has nonetheless become a legend in his own lifetime. From the barrios of a Havana slum and a history of young delinquency which brought him several times in line with the law, he now conquers the world's stages performing before royalty and rulers, and winning hearts and plaudits for his exacting technique and the breathtaking, fearless risks he takes in his dancing. Along with his exceptional physical talents, his friendliness, interest in others and good manners have resulted in him being sought out for chat shows and interviews, while there is always a throng of loyal fans outside stage doors waiting for him after a performance.

He has known as many lows as highs in his lifetime and yet, pushed on by a paternal force, he learned dutifully to develop and share his talent with the world. For Carlos, who remains one of the nicest and most humble stars in today's artistic galaxy, it has been an unbelievable but wonderfully enriching journey, and his life offers a story of hope to all.

1

From Barrio Bajo to Ballet Barre

'Tethering the little slum ruffian'

IT WAS GOOD that he was bad. If he had not been a rebel, a delinquent skipping school to breakdance and play football, he might have ended up as a truck driver like his father, or become one of the many job-less young men, lounging around on street corners. Or even worse, he could have landed in prison.

But Carlos Acosta had a destiny to play out, one that would take him from anonymity, loneliness and the sultry heat of his home slums, to adulation, fame and fortune on the stages of the world where he has become one of the most famous male dancers of his generation. However, it was because of his constant truancy that his father sent him to be disciplined in the ballet studio. And the rest, as they say, is history,

even though the decision didn't produce an immediate magical about-face as happens in many of the
fairy-tale ballets that Carlos has since danced. He had
to learn to love classical ballet – and that took many,
many years of hard work and resistance to its tough
demanding disciplines. He would have preferred to
take the easy route and just be 'normal'.

Carlos Junior Acosta Quesada was born on 2 June
1973 in Los Pinos, in the Arroyo Naranjo district of
La Habana, on the sleeping crocodile-shaped Caribbean island of Cuba. Today, parts of Los Pinos boast
a burgeoning tourist area with modern villas overlooking white sands and turquoise seas. But for Carlos in the 1970s, it was a grim place to be brought up
in. Los Pinos, typical of so many other neighbour-
hoods in Cuba, was drab and dusty with crumbling
brickwork falling onto cracked and broken paths.
Women, intent on finding food for their families,
scurried along these litter-filled pavements trying to
ignore the rotting smells from overflowing garbage
bins which attracted not only clouds of flies but feral
cats and mangy, homeless dogs. Ramshackle trucks
rattled noisily along the pot-holed roads, kicking up
dust and throwing out fumes. Despite their perilous
appearance, these metal monstrosities were beloved
by their owners and tenderly repaired with parts from
old, rusty Russian machines left during the friend-
lier days between these two once-strong bastions of

communism. 'They would also be repaired with bent coat hangers, bits of wire, TV remote control parts – whatever you could lay your hands on', laughed Carlos. 'It was a wonder that they moved at all, but to own one, was to have status.'

The Acosta family lived on the upper floor of a two-storey rural wooden house in one of these bustling dusty streets – Naranjito 971 e/Fernandez, Castro y Avenida los Pinos. There were six apartments in this old building, three down and three up. The Acostas reached their apartment via a rusting metal staircase that branched off to the left and to the right near the top. 'We were in the middle apartment,' he said, 'and we usually went up the left side and passed the window of our neighbours. Everyone knew what was going on with us. I was really happy here as a kid despite us not having anything. I miss the atmosphere even today.' The Acostas had no running water and Carlos relates in his autobiography that every drop had to be carried in by hand and up the stairs, while the walls throughout the apartment had cracks that let in the daylight and overwhelming heat, and gave cosy shelter to the many bugs.* The challenge to keep everything clean in the dust and the heat was depressing, yet Cuban women are house-proud, none more so than Carlos' mother who daily would

---

* Carlos Acosta. *No Way Home*. HarperPress, 2007, p.6

sweep away the dirt and grime and go on her knees to scrub the rough floors. There was no privacy in these shanty-like homes – everyone knew everybody's business, and every sound of neighbours' activities and conflicts, together with the noises of gear-grinding trucks and spluttering motorbikes on the road outside had to be tolerated day and night. Sleeping accommodation for the family of five in the Acosta household was equally bleak. When he was three years old, Carlos' parents divorced but, due to the economic situation, his father continued to live in the same house. 'He didn't talk much. He was very strict and hard on us so it was a traumatic childhood for me and my sisters,' he remembered. With just two rooms and the large, ungainly pieces of battered furniture that inhabited the meagre space, the family had to be divided at bedtime: his father slept on a mat in the living room while the two sisters slept squashed together in an antiquated double bed whose springs poked through the well-worn mattress. Little Carlos slept with his mother in a single bed that was shoved up against the wall. But like young children, he was happy there: 'It was home. We had two rabbits that just hopped around the apartment. I am not sure if they were bought for me as pets, or to multiply for food, but they were part of my young life,' he recalled years later in London. 'Up on the roof I kept pigeons. I raised them and bonded with them. You have to put them in wire pens so that they can see the sky around them and get to know their home territory. And I would fly them. You know that pigeons try to pull other pigeons down into their area, so if one landed on my roof and I caught it, then it belonged to me. Their owners often offered to pay to get it back. I had around six pigeons and they became my confidantes whenever I was troubled – or, more often, in trouble. I would go up to the roof to get away from the problems in my house – it was the only place where I could be alone and hide. I developed a nice bond with them.' Up there on the flat rooftop, their gentle cooing would put his world to rights for that brief moment.

From the mid-sixteenth century, shiploads of slaves were brought over from sub-Saharan Africa to the verdant island of Cuba to work in the coffee and later sugar cane plantations of the rich settlers in this Spanish colony. Over the years the races intermarried so that today's Cuba is peopled by a mixed and vibrant race whose skin colour ranges from European white to African ebony, with all the hues in between. In Cuba there is generally no prejudice and the people live in harmony with each other, though Carlos thinks differently. 'Discrimination is very subtle and it is never reprimanded. Someone in the street will call out "hey Negrito" to get your attention. But you would never hear, "hey brunette," "hey blonde". It should be taught in schools not to differentiate between people, but sadly it isn't.'

Cuba's melting pot of races often produces a spectrum of colours in a single family. Carlos' family was no exception. His maternal grandfather, after whom Carlos had been named, had Spanish forebears and was fair-haired with green eyes, so Carlos' mother, María, and all her family were white-skinned, as was his older half-sister Berthe who had been born out of wedlock. His second sister Marilin was a *mulata criolla*, with an olive skin, but Carlos took after their father Pedro, a direct descendant of African slaves who had very dark skin, and though Carlos was somewhat lighter in colour, he shared his father's wild, tight, curly Afro hair and wide nose. For him, right from an early age, being black was, and continued to be, a thorn in his flesh. It was a constant nagging torment that continued to haunt his confidence for much of his life, especially in his early days as a dancer in the traditionally white world of classical ballet. Sadly, this colour prejudice even ran with some of his closest, pale-skinned family members, as Carlos discovered during his early childhood.

Born in 1918, Pedro Acosta's own mother – Carlos' paternal grandmother – had been born on a sugar plantation, the daughter of slaves. Pedro said little about his father who died when he was six years old, but Carlos did learn that Acosta was not a family name. In the tradition of those days of servitude, slaves took on the surname of their master, in this case Acosta. Losing his father at such an early age meant that young Pedro had to grow up quickly and take on the responsibilities of helping to provide for his mother and a younger brother. To augment the family's meagre finances, he soon found a job selling newspapers. He later worked at the dockside as a stevedore, loading heavy canvas bags of sugar, which, at that time in its history, was Cuba's great export, due to a sugar shortage in Europe caused by the First World War. In the 1920s, the island of Cuba had become a tropical paradise, playing host to many pleasure-seeking individuals. It was seen as a fantastic playground for the rich with a reputation for 'anything goes'. Life on the lush island was invigorating for those with money in their pockets. But for others, it resulted in great inequality between the rich and the poor. The divided atmosphere also brought discrimination between black and white, something that Pedro had to face on a daily basis. The blacks did the menial tasks, working as shoeshine boys, street cleaners and stevedores and were regularly humiliated and even beaten. Segregation was a way of life just as it was in America's Deep South. But, reports Carlos, on one occasion Pedro memorably beat the system.* It was a just moment, a very brief one and one unbeknown to him at the time, that was to change the course of his future son's life forever. He'd snuck into a 'whites only' cinema and sat gazing at the screen in amazement and incredulity at a silent film, seeing for the first time in his life, the mystical beauty of ballet dancers twirling gracefully. Their actions seemed almost magical and the splendour of it all entranced him. But he didn't get to watch for long. His presence was quickly noted and the management unceremoniously booted him out. However, the images of those precious moments, which Pedro did not understand and which he never encountered again or analysed, remained dormant in his mind during the ensuing forty-odd years.

Carlos' mother was the eldest of three daughters – María, Mireya and Lucía – of philanthropic Carlos Quesada and his wife Georgina. However, the pretty, blonde, vivacious and single María found herself pregnant at the age of seventeen and in 1965 gave birth to a daughter, Berthe. Eighteen months later, much to the family's displeasure she met and fell in love with Pedro Acosta, a man nearly three times her age, who had been married three times before and had already fathered eight children. With María, he added three more, the youngest being Carlos, who

---

* *No Way Home*, p.9

came into this world via a difficult Caesarean section, due to his, now famous, feet wrongly positioned to come out first.

The Acosta home-life was typical of those who lived in the run-down neighbourhood. The average wage at that time was around seventy pesos and mothers would spend their days in queues in the blazing sunshine trying to find food for the family. Each Cuban family member was given a ration book, which allowed provisions to be bought at subsidised prices. The food was distributed at the local store or *bodega* and was usually of poor quality. Each person was allowed a certain allocation every month of rice, fish, beans, potatoes, soaps and detergents, though whether those products could be found was another matter. If you had the money there was the free market where fresh items were always available but more expensive. Or there were stores where – if you were entitled to have them – you paid with American dollars. The Acosta family did not have access to these shops, so they had to rely on the state stores and hope that there was something left when they reached the counter. Pedro worked as a driver travelling around the small island delivering fruit in a battered old green Soviet Zil 59 lorry. He was often away for up to a month at a time, which meant that his absences would stretch the family's food allowance a little further, and sometimes he would return home with leftover supplies which augmented the Acosta family's meagre diet. Like other women, María would often go into the countryside with a bag of essentials, such as soap, toothpaste and cleaning products that she had bought with her ration card, to exchange them for fresh food. But her children were always hungry – especially Carlos.

The Acostas often had little on their own meal plates but small portions of precious food could be found elsewhere in the home. Pedro was a follower of Santería, an Afro-Cuban religion based on the Yoruba culture in Nigeria and brought over by slaves. The traditions incorporate the worship of *orishas* – multidimensional beings which represent the forces of nature. Pedro would pray to these saints regularly and leave offerings for them. These would include valued amounts of fruit, cakes and sweets which, apart from attracting flies as they decayed, would make the children's mouths drool with envy when their own plates were empty. Followers of Santería believe that the spirits will give them help in life, if they carry out the appropriate rituals, some of which involve animal sacrifice. During Carlos' childhood, his father's shrine to the saints was set up in the living room – a collection of strange metallic items on top of which stood a small statue of a cockerel. If the bird fell over, it meant that something terrible was about to happen. Many times during normal childish play, the statue would tumble, causing Carlos great panic. Carefully he would set it upright again and then warily watch his father when he returned home for any telltale signs that he might discover his son's misdemeanour. On one unforgettable day, Carlos came home to find that his pet rabbits, Negrito and Canela, had found their way up to the shrine and had nibbled at the gifts for the saints. He quickly patched up the mess they had made, praying that his father wouldn't notice. Nothing was said but a few days later there was the rare treat of meat on the Acostas' table for supper. The children tucked in excitedly – only later to discover that it was rabbit meat! The pets had duly received their punishment. 'I was so upset,' Carlos reported, 'I have never eaten rabbit meat again!'

The three maternal sisters were very close and would visit each other regularly but from a very early age, Carlos became aware of his relatives' light skin colourings, and his difference troubled him, especially when Aunt Mireya would give all her attention to fair-haired Berthe. Fortunately Aunt Lucía made a special effort to include the other two darker children. Yet throughout his childhood and subsequent life, Carlos has held warm feelings for each and every member of his family, with the initial exception of his father – that loyalty, love and gratitude would only come later in his life. Pedro he feared, for his father had a violent temper and would lash out physically when Carlos was in trouble, especially later in his childhood when he was discovered skipping ballet classes to play football with his friends.

Nevertheless, the bond of family in the Acosta household remained very strong despite the many challenges it faced and would face. As his life progressed, Carlos began to realise the reasons for his father's strict and often forceful conduct towards him. Pedro was trying to instil in his son the fact that when you have a talent, you have a duty to develop it, no matter what problems are thrown at you, and that the only way to achieve is through hard, often gruelling work. Pedro's coldness and cruelty had been to awaken the young boy from the lackadaisical dream of just living, to a sense of striving. His father's lack of demonstrative love and his physical severity hurt him emotionally for many years, but gradually, as he has developed and succeeded, Carlos has come to see that it was the only way out of his mentally fenced-in surroundings. He now holds up his father as one of the greatest men he has known.

In 1959 the bushy-bearded, army-capped Fidel Castro overthrew General Fulgencio Batista and came to power. By 1960 all opposition was culled, controversial newspapers were closed, and radio and TV came under state control. Then in 1961 came the unsuccessful attempt at the Bay of Pigs by American

CIA-trained, anti-Castro Cubans to overthrow the government. The following year saw the Cuban Missile Crisis after which America broke all diplomatic relations with the country. Embargoes were imposed and all American commercial and financial trading stopped. Life under the strict communist regime now became wrought with severe hardships, especially famine. A travel ban was also inflicted on the people. The enormous challenges continued despite the economic and practical help the country now received from the Soviet Union, which needed communist Cuba as an important base for its activities in South America, just as much as Cuba needed the trade and finance. But when the early rumblings of discontent in the Iron Curtain countries began, and continued to crescendo until the fall of the Berlin Wall in 1989, that support was taken from Cuba, leaving them to struggle on their own once more.

During the hardest period of the embargoes, with the scarcity of food and money due to the lack of trade, many Cubans opted to take their lives into their own hands to start a new life in America. They would unofficially set sail in small boats and homemade rafts, many of which capsized on the treacherous waters of the Florida Strait. Then unexpectedly, from April to October in 1980, Fidel Castro temporarily lifted the restrictions that had prevented his people from leaving their homeland. It was called the

Mariel Boat Lift and 1.2 million nationals took advantage of the opportunity.*

The Acostas, including María's close family, were not exempt from wishing to leave. The lack of food and goods and the seemingly no way out of their poverty was enough to tempt everyone to believe that life would be better elsewhere. They had relatives in Venezuela and these family members could obtain exit papers for them all to go there first. From there, the Acosta/Quesada clan could then formally request to go to America to start a new life in Miami. So they all applied for exit permits.

When Carlos was seven, Grandma Georgina, his two aunts, and young cousin came to live with Pedro, María, Berthe, Marilin and him while they waited for their invitations to leave. With the paltry wages of a truck driver, it was hard enough to provide for one's own growing offspring. Now suddenly the Acostas' food allowance had to be stretched even further, as indeed did the four walls of their small home. Tragically, during the waiting, his kindly, twenty-six-year-old Aunt Lucía developed schizophrenia, was admitted to hospital and then took her own life. It shocked the family but made them all the more determined to seek a new life abroad. When the papers that would allow them to apply for

---

* www.globalsecurity.org

a visa finally arrived from their Venezuelan relatives, everyone's name was included on it – except for the darker-skinned members, in other words, Pedro, Carlos and Marilin. All María's dreams for a new, less burdensome life together with her closest kin were shattered. While her papers and Berthe's were in order and they were free to leave, her husband and two other children had been left off the list. What and how was she to choose: a new, hopefully brighter future with family members in another country, but without two of her children and any financial support from her husband? Or should she stay and continue her present life of drudgery in Cuba with all of its problems? With a heavy heart, she decided to stay, and watched in disbelief when the day finally came and her mother and sisters set off, with very little hopes of ever being together again. María would never get over the shock of being left behind.

Carlos was a real little ruffian of the streets. Known in the neighbourhood as Yuli, a name that Berthe had given him, his days were filled playing with the local lads and following their wayward ways. He still loves to tell how, at an early age, he learned to scale the neighbours' walls and steal mangoes from the trees – and not just to satiate an ever-present hunger. He would also sell the stolen fruit to the local shop, using the money to go to the cinema. Swift and smart, it was rare for him to be caught but when that happened, he would be severely reprimanded and often beaten by his father. Undeterred and promising to repent, he'd soon be off on his thieving rounds again. When he was five years old, he started at kindergarten – 'it was called the Granma School', he reported – near to his home. He set off each day in a clean white shirt, red shorts and later, the traditional blue pioneer scarf around his neck. But the young boy felt that school was a rude interruption to his life on the streets.

Like all young boys, his passion was football. He dreamed of being on the local team and when talent spotters came around, he would perform all kinds of exertions to show that he was fit, hoping to impress them. But to his great disappointment, he was never chosen. Marilin was interested in disco dancing and showed him lots of the moves, which he picked up quickly. When he was nearly nine, breakdancing became the craze in Cuba and with it came the body-popping, moon-walking moves of Michael Jackson. 'Michael had branched out from the Jackson Five to start his solo career with Quincy Jones,' says Carlos. 'Man, it was a great time. Jackson was one of the biggest influences on me when I was growing up.'

All the youngsters were in awe of the American singer and dancer and tried to emulate him. Someone in the neighbourhood would see Jackson performing his latest pop song on television and then show off the

incredible dance steps to the local youngsters. Everyone wanted to dance like Michael Jackson, especially
Carlos. 'Michael Jackson was my idol,' he said. 'He
made it big time and I wanted to be like him, to move
and to dance like him. He had personality as well as
enormous talent. He brought a revolution to dance
worldwide and all of us kids tried to do his moves.
We loved him and would learn every step and copy
him. His death [in 2009] was a huge shock and it has
deprived the world of a great artist. I felt really bad
when I heard the news. He still had so much more
to say and do.' Carlos' sister Marilin joined a local
breakdancing group and showed herself an excellent exponent of this new craze. She often let her little brother come along and he'd watch with interest.
Unknown to her, when she was at school, he'd play
truant and go back to learn more moves from the
street gang who had formed a club called Vieja Línea.
The fashion was baggy pants and sweatshirts, topped
off with a cap turned back-to-front, a headwear fashion statement that Carlos still adopts, though today,
shiny, bouncy curls tumble out in coiffured abandon
unlike the tangled matted hair then. And they would
chomp on ersatz chewing gum – sticking plaster – 'to
give us "attitude"', chuckled Carlos. Young Yuli was a
natural from an early age, throwing himself into head
rolls and shoulder spins with gusto – something he
still can do today. Marilin was amazed at his progress

and natural talent, unaware, as was his family also, that he had been skipping school to practise with the boys. His breakdance partner was a sprightly young lad called Opito and they polished their moves until they were good enough to compete in local competitions. Carlos was given the name of *El Moro de Los Pinos* (the Moor of Los Pinos) and found that in dancing, he became someone else, fearless and no longer shy. At one competition, he won his first trophy and he suddenly felt that life was beginning to look up. He was happy. Life was good for the nine-year-old, so he believed – but not for long. His father thought otherwise.

When Pedro found out that his son had been missing school to go off breakdancing, he realised that something had to be done to discipline the unruly lad who was well on the road, even at this early age, to becoming a hooligan in trouble with the law. But all of Pedro's threats, warnings and even physical punishments seemed to have no effect on his young son. No sooner had Carlos recovered from his chastisements, than he would be back to his old unreformed ways with his gang. His father was at his wits' end as to how to tame him.

And then by chance, Pedro met a downstairs neighbour who told him that her two sons were studying at the Alejo Carpentier Provincial School of Ballet. Her words rekindled a flame in him. Suddenly the long-buried remembrance of the dancers in that early flickering black-and-white film, rose up once more in his consciousness, like a metamorphosed dragonfly escaping from the murky depths of its stagnant life with promises of a new future in a world of elegance and grace.

Ballet!

That's what his delinquent young son needed – discipline in the form of ballet classes. That would keep him in line and off the streets. And there would also be other advantages. Not only would he be educated and trained for free, but he would also receive food during the training – and he had a rapacious appetite – thus cutting down on household bills. When the unsuspecting nine-year-old came home later that day, both parents were eagerly awaiting to tell him the good news about his exciting new future. Carlos' reaction was expectedly explosive and he lashed out verbally. He knew nothing about ballet except that he'd heard it was for 'poofs'. If he followed his parents' wishes, he would lose his status in the gang and become the laughing stock of the whole neighbourhood. He would not be obedient and go. But his father was adamant.

A week later, María dragged her unwilling son on the long trip on three overcrowded ramshackle buses to get to the downtown district of Vedado in Havana. The ballet school was situated at the intersection of streets L and 19 where Carlos joined a queue of young hopefuls and their pushy parents, some of whom looked contemptuously at the pretty blonde mother and her dark brooding child. Again Carlos had the sensation of being a second-class citizen because he was not white. Once inside and stripped to his tattered and grubby swimming pants, he was stretched and pulled like a ball of putty as the ballet staff evaluated his physique and future growth, rather than his ability to dance. They could mould him to their requirements during the years of rigorous training, but not if his body was going to grow up wrongly or if he wasn't naturally supple. A musical test followed, then he was asked to improvise a dance. Puzzled, he decided to do the only thing he knew how to do – breakdance. Suddenly he was on the floor, throwing himself about, body popping like Michael Jackson until the incredulous judges called for him to stop before he did himself an injury. Content that he had shown himself an unlikely candidate, he and his mother returned home again on the three-bus journey and waited for the dreaded letter from the school. A week later it came and so did the realisation of Carlos' worst fears – he'd been accepted to start next term in August 1982. He raced up to the roof – his sanctuary from all the problems he was about to face – to tell his pet pigeons his awful news.

2

Discipline, Distractions and Disasters Spell Truancy

'Slow, boring steps'

GOING TO BALLET SCHOOL meant routine and now Carlos' day began at five a.m. when he would wake, wash, have a drink of milky coffee (or just sugar water when the coffee ran out), and set off to catch the three rickety buses to the centre of Havana – only about nine miles away as the crow flies and a forty-minute car ride. 'But for me, it took hours, since I had to change buses and wait for the next one, battle to get on, and be squashed by all the sweaty people as the bus rambled around every street. It was very stressful,' said Carlos. However, the hot sticky journey opened up a new world to his eyes when he finally got off the bus in the centre of town. There the results of affluence could be seen on the streets and in the capital's fancy hotels and pristine swimming pools. But there was no time to stand and stare. Now he had two schools to attend. Academic classes started at eight o'clock and continued until noon and for those, he had to go to the Orlando Pantoja School three blocks away from the ballet studios. There he joined 200 students, of whom only fifty were enrolled at the ballet school. In his own academic class there were just two ballet students and he constantly found himself the victim of bullying and name-calling by the other boys. Instinctively, he would revert to his street upbringing and fight back, which always got him in trouble. The afternoons at the Alejo Carpentier Provincial School of Ballet were given over to dancing and his first snail-paced and accuracy-demanding ballet class convinced him that he was definitely in the wrong place. To start with, the boys had to wear leotards just like the girls (although they wore their trunks on top), then, when he went into the studio, he was shown classical ballet's five basic positions of the arms and feet, had to turn his feet out like a penguin and follow a few elementary steps, all of them with French names. The class was long – an hour and fifteen minutes – horrendously repetitive, slow and monotonous, and the whole thing filled the young boy with gloom. The deliberate sloth-like pacing of their training was to develop strong technique and muscular control but its very lack of action made Carlos quickly disinterested. The thought then of daily following the same boring schedule made him feel trapped and he longed to escape back to his breakdance world of free expression – and naturally his football too. Little did he realise as he executed those first simple ballet exercises over and over, that he would be starting out each and every day for the next thirty years of his life with these same slow, boring (to him), repetitive steps as does every classical dancer – professional and student – around the globe. As with his academic school, there were twenty students in his ballet class and he quickly noticed that only two were black – he being one of them. He was thankful when the bell finally rang, and he raced off to the canteen for his lunch. The food was good, though he could have eaten twice as much, and revived him and he began to feel that perhaps things weren't all bad – the food, at least, was an incentive to come back. After lunch, there were other classes – French language, historical dance and piano lessons – which continued until six p.m. Then Carlos would set out on his many buses home – all of them over-flowing with hot and weary passengers – to arrive around nine thirty, exhausted. As if to remind him of what might have been, had he had a different father, he would often see his old street gang performing to crowds of admiring people. He would pull back into the shadows and sneak past so no one would see him and taunt him, even though he was constantly being told at school that there was no stigma to being a male ballet dancer. He knew that didn't hold sway with his butch street mates. After a quick meal, he was ready for bed exhausted – that five o'clock alarm came all too quickly.

Carlos, who was known as Junior at the ballet school, unenthusiastically continued for six months, then one night he returned home to find that his dear mother had had a stroke and was in hospital. The emotional strain and stress she had been bottling up since her own mother and sisters left the country for America, finally had taken its toll and now there was a possibility that she might not live. Carlos' whole world seemed to collapse around him. Afraid and lonely, he finally fell into a deep sleep and woke to find his father had already left for work. He quickly got himself ready and set off for school. But he was tired mentally and physically and, unable to concentrate on his academic lessons, kept dropping off to sleep in class. One teacher who was always kind and friendly to him and whom in return, he idolised, recognised his challenging home life and took pity on him. She listened to his sad tale, showing the compassion and hope that he so desperately needed. When he had mumps later in his school days, she would come out to his house and coach him. 'I have very fond feelings for her. She was called Nancy and was someone special in my early life,' Carlos recalled many years later. Nancy allowed Carlos time off from his classes to visit his mother the next day and he was shocked by her changed appearance. Her head had been shaved for the operation to remove a brain tumour. She looked years older and so frail.

Back at the apartment, Pedro took over the cooking chores, despite having had no experience, and the children suffered in silence with his poor efforts, fearful of complaining and consequent reprisals. The strain was evident in every one of them. At this time, Carlos himself had an accident in class when a metal *barre* collapsed and made a deep wound in his neck. He was told to take two weeks of rest, which suited him fine – he now had official permission to escape his monotonous ballet life. Perhaps this accident would soften his father's heart and he would listen to his son's pleas to lead a normal boy's life, and allow him to return to the neighbourhood school, to his friends, his dreams of football and also to breakdancing. However, unknown to Carlos, the ballet school had told Pedro earlier that, though his boy was lazy, he had talent. Now Pedro was more determined than ever for him to continue with his training and not become like one of the layabouts visible on every dusty street corner. When Carlos dared to raise the topic again with his father, his pleas were met with physical force as Pedro told his young son not to contemplate any other way of life. So, as soon as his neck wound healed, it was back to ballet school with a heavy heart and sinking feeling of entrapment.

The ever-reluctant Carlos continued the repetitive daily routine and soon his first year was drawing to a close. As always, the school was to hold its annual end-of-year concert at the Teatro Nacional de Cuba in downtown Havana and he was chosen to dance a Polish mazurka with a pretty young girl called Grettel. Again he was mentally aware of their differences – she was light-skinned and refined, he still uncouth with wild bushy hair and lazy local lingo, which showed he came from the wrong side of town. But a smile from her produced results and Carlos, with love in his young heart, danced with feeling. When the mazurka was over and the applause rang out, he realised to his amazement that he had enjoyed himself. He certainly was pleased about the reception he had received and he felt elated about what he had accomplished. Perhaps there was something to this dancing stuff after all, he thought. But sadly the feeling didn't last long. As other families greeted their offspring afterwards on the street, congratulating them and taking them off to celebrate, the fact that none of his family had come to see him dance cut to the heart and his great sense of loneliness and displacement reared its head again. He trudged through the happy throng to get to the bus stop for his long journey home, truly despondent. 'It was awful,' he reported later. Arriving very late, he walked straight into his old gang who taunted him with unkind names and proceeded to joke cruelly about his mother's condition. This was the last straw for the young boy and sparked off the fighter in him. He struck out, only to be the loser against so many. After an evening that had given him his first taste of success in the spotlight and should have given him great joy, he crawled home bruised and swollen, feeling very sorry for himself. Then he heard the news that his mother would be home within the week, and joy overcame the pain. 'We children took the day off from school to clean the house and bring in provisions for her return,' Carlos remembered. María, still looking deathly ill, was brought back by ambulance and put in her bed where she would stay for many weeks. But kindly neighbours rallied round to help care for her and cook food for the children.

With the family together again, things began to return to normal and it wasn't long before Carlos felt the pull of life outside the ballet studios once more. One morning, he left home at his usual time but set off on a different bus in another direction. It took him to the stadium where a young football team trained and he desperately hoped that he might get chosen to play. He hung around until the boys arrived and was delighted when he was allowed to join them. He played well and received the promise that he could come back anytime. Then they returned to their school, leaving Carlos to plot the rest of his day. Since it was only midday, he could neither go off to the ballet studios nor go home, so he just lazed around until the normal time for his homecoming. He managed to successfully lie to his father about what he'd done that day, and when he realised that he could get away with not going to ballet school, he grew bolder still and began regularly to miss school. He was oblivious to the fact that, sooner or later, the school would contact his family, and when the call came, so did the expected results. Pedro was summoned to a meeting with the teachers and told that his son had been absent from school for nearly four weeks. At first he said there must be some mistake – didn't he see his son set off each morning to catch the bus? Then he was told that the truancy had been going on throughout the year and that, because he had missed so much, his son would not be cast in any of the school productions. With the news, Pedro nearly exploded and when Carlos, who had spent another good day bunking off school, walked in as nonchalantly as possible that evening at his usual time, his father was waiting for him. Carlos could see by the pent-up, ready-to-erupt expression that his truancy had been discovered. When he again tried to lie to his father about his activities, he was hit so hard that he was sent flying across the room. Then he saw that his father had picked up a machete but fortunately his two sisters were holding him back and screaming at their brother, telling him to run as fast as he could. He set off over the rooftops fearing for his life and not knowing where he was going. Finally he arrived in Vieja Linda, an insalubrious part of town where Eddie, a twenty-three-year-old acquaintance from his breakdancing days took the frightened nine-year-old in until the storm was over. Carlos returned home some days later much to his mother's great relief, while his father remained silent and ignored him.

In his second year of study, ten-year-old-Carlos made an attempt to work harder and his father was pleased with the good reports that he was now getting from the teachers and a slightly better, if somewhat restrained, relationship between father and son was developing. However, returning home early one afternoon due, not this time with plans for skiving off, but the genuine illness of a teacher, Carlos noticed a crowd around his home. His uplifted mood quickly changed and his heart pounded loudly. Certain that his mother must have had another turn, he broke into a run fearing the worst. And the worst it was, though this time it was his father. Driving home from work Pedro had stopped at a red light before turning.

As the light readied to change and he began to set off, a motorbike and sidecar raced past and crashed into the truck. The two passengers on the bike were unhurt but the woman in the sidecar was caught by the impact and killed. Despite Pedro's clean licence and complete innocence of the offence, the penalty for causing death was two years in a state penitentiary and he was sent to one on the other side of Havana that housed murderers and thugs. 'We were all traumatised with the news but I was very young and simply didn't know what it meant,' said Carlos. We were all generally afraid of my father – he was unpredictable and temperamental and when things didn't go his way, we didn't know what would spark him off. But this was serious. However, it now crossed my mind that since he was not at home anymore, I could finally do whatever I wanted. One thing I knew – I certainly didn't want to be a ballet dancer.' Carlos was torn – he did not want to cause more trouble for his family but he was still finding it hard to be caged into ballet routines. Deep down he knew that to go against his father's commands was dangerous.

The fatherless Acosta home managed as best it could but without a regular income coming in, it was tough going. Pedro was later transferred to another detention centre where he was able to work and earn a little money and that helped feed the huge appetite of the fast-growing boy. Carlos knew he had to support his mother as best he could during this difficult time – she was still weak and unable to do anything in the home – so he tried to be a good student and not get into trouble. He helped at home by washing his own clothes but his daily exertions in the terrific heat made him sweaty, and being inexperienced at household duties, it was hard for him to get the body odour out of his clothing, giving his classmates and teachers a new reason to pick on him. Humiliated and embarrassed, the flame of inferiority and worthlessness resurfaced and he once more started skipping school. He had tried his hardest to knuckle down when his father had first gone away, and had surprised his teachers with his concentration and hard work. They thought him a transformed student and he was given a role in one of the teacher's ballets. Then had come the taunting, and his consequent absenteeism resulted in his name being taken off the list of students who were to appear in the important National Festival of Schools in the beautiful historic town of Camagüey. This was a hard blow to Carlos as it was something he had been looking forward to very much. It would have been a chance to see another part of his country with the added opportunity of watching other students perform. Instead, he had to stay behind and it was especially hard for him to hear later that the trip had turned out to be highly successful for the school. The students returned with many prizes and high recognition of their work, and they talked of meeting other young people from other schools. Carlos had missed out again.

The end-of-year concert for pupils of the Alejo Carpentier Provincial School of Ballet was to be held this time at the famous García Lorca auditorium in the Gran Teatro in the centre of Havana. Carlos constantly amazed his teachers with his ability to catch up with the class even though he was still regularly playing truant. Perhaps it was a clever ploy by them for, though they were not pleased with his behaviour, they had cast him in the show to encourage him to work for they could see that there was hidden talent that needed to be developed. He was to dance the mazurka again with Grettel, which this time didn't go down well with either of them. Despite that earlier success on stage, he was again unsettled by thoughts of feeling trapped in this unwanted life. On the day of the performance, he told his mother that he had a holiday, and after sleeping for most of the morning, set off in search of his local friends at the very time he should have been preparing to go to the theatre. Wearing torn and outgrown shorts and running barefoot, he met up with his friends who were surprised and delighted to see him. He was back with his pack again doing all the things that his ballet classmates would frown on. The fun and games soon turned into a friendly mud-slinging fight and before long they were all filthy but happy. Carlos was having such a great time being a normal local lad again that he was unaware that a car had pulled up near to them. The next thing he heard was an authoritative voice shouting 'Junior, Junior', his school name. Since his friends only knew him as Yuli, they all stopped, curious to know who was being called. Suddenly Carlos was yanked and shoved, mud and all, into the car by his irate ballet teacher. The car sped through the rough potholed streets of Havana, tossing its occupants back and forth. Carlos was informed that, since his mazurka was the first dance of the evening, the theatre was delaying the performance for thirty minutes, so he had better be prepared. Once at the theatre, hands appeared from everywhere, stripping him, scrubbing at the mud, rubbing his face sore, putting make-up on and thrusting him into his costume. Then he was pushed onto the stage as the curtain rose and he danced the mazurka with a very grumpy Grettel – she'd been waiting and waiting for him to turn up. This time, he received no heartwarming smiles from her.

3

Expulsion and Epiphany

'Wanting for the first time to succeed'

IT WAS NOW SEPTEMBER 1984 and eleven-year-old Carlos found that he had to repeat his second year at the ballet school as he had started at the age of nine rather than the usual ten years. Now he was in a class with his own age group, which should have been easier for him. But the bullying that he had become accustomed to with his older fellow students did not miraculously stop. So neither did his truancy. With such constant name-calling as *Junior del Desastre (Junior the Disaster)* it appeared clear-cut to him that his new classmates disliked him. The lack of friends here was often unbearable and staying away from ballet school seemed the only recourse. With no one he could turn to for advice, he found that he just could not be comfortable in that stifling and acidic atmosphere. To cage such a free spirit in the ultra-disciplined world of ballet was expecting a miracle and it wasn't long before Carlos again found every opportunity to bunk off school to join his old street friends, whom he knew would treat him well, especially when they realised that he had escaped from the prissy ballet school to come back to them. Without his father around to constantly check on him, he felt liberated enough to get away with it and his absences from school grew more frequent. His mother María was called regularly about her son's failure to show up for classes, but her description of their fatherless home, her illness, the challenges now to make ends meet without Pedro's salary and her tearful pleas touched the teachers and they would give the young boy yet another chance. While ballet was still not what he wanted, Carlos learned to lie very well about it. Whenever he made the regular family visits to see his father, he would make up stories about how well he was doing in his ballet classes, and tell of all the successes he'd had, especially on the school trip to Camagüey, when the truth was that he had actually been banned from going.

When he entered his third year at school, Carlos told his father that he had been made head of the student group, though in reality he was despised and mocked by most of his peers. Pedro seemed pleased with his son's good news that the teaching staff was recognising him for his hard work. He must have thought that he had been right all along and that the discipline of ballet school had been the answer to all Carlos' problems. His tenacious stern decision had turned his son's life around so that he would not grow up to be like the other boys on the block who had no focus beyond their delinquent lives. Their futures would be on the streets, tempted by drugs and crime and that was not what he wanted for his son. Eventually Pedro was released and returned home to his family, and, most importantly, to his beloved saints, to whom he immediately made sacrifices. Family life was going to be much easier and more peaceful from now on since his son had finally settled down in ballet school.

But it wasn't long before Pedro got a phone call asking him to come to the school. Anticipating it to be a meeting extolling his son's progress and admirable achievements (as he had been told by Carlos) his mouth dropped wide open at the report he was now getting from the staff. Pedro heard in no uncertain terms how Carlos was constantly playing truant, had missed the school trip to the Camagüey Festival (rather than having the successes that he had related to his father), and had failed what few exams he actually had taken through sheer laziness. The staff at the school had now discussed his work and had come to the conclusion that there was going to be no way that he could be re-admitted next term. As far as they were concerned, Carlos' training to become a classical ballet dancer had ended. He was not welcome back in the school.

His son expelled! With a face like thunder, Pedro dragged the boy home and once they were back in the house, thrashed him within an inch of his life. His mother and sister screamed and feared for his being but Carlos survived the angry beating, finally managing to escape his father's clutches, battered, bruised and thoroughly chastened. From then on, life in the Acosta household continued cautiously, though for Carlos, 'it was like treading on eggshells to be in the house with my father'. The topic of ballet was not raised and fortunately for Carlos, Pedro suddenly became more and more involved in his religion and his display of saints. He bought ever-increasing quantities of food to place on the altar, spending any spare money on them, while not eating himself. Carlos was secretly pleased that he had been turned out of ballet school at the age of just thirteen and so could become a normal boy again, but he knew that Pedro still held on to his long treasured dreams for his son. One day when he could no longer bear the tension that pervaded the household, the young boy summoned up all his courage and faced his father. Bravely stating that he wasn't happy studying ballet, he pleaded to be allowed to give it up. But Pedro scoffed at him. Happiness, he told the boy, was not something you could or should depend on; it was something you had to constantly seek in life. 'The look on his face and the remembrance of my past punishments showed me that that was the end of the discussion,' recalled Carlos. There seemed no way to escape his father's fantasies, even though the young ballet dancer had no school to go to after the summer holidays.

A few weeks later, it seemed as though Pedro's increased religious fervour had paid off. A letter came from the school informing him that, due to the fact that so many students that year had failed their exams, his son was included in the list of pupils to return to school to re-sit them. This was devastating news for Carlos though he knew he had to do his best. But, even if he did well this time in the exam, there was always going to be the question of how to keep him tied up in school for the full day when he was so wily and nimble in finding ways to escape. All of his teachers were fed up with his past behaviour, complaining that it disrupted their teaching and the general morale of the school and would gladly be rid of him. They all agreed that, while he certainly had a talent for dancing, his lack of dedication and truancy were wasting it as well as the school's time and efforts. It became obvious that nobody wanted him back, even after he had managed to scrape through the exams and thus was eligible to move up to the next grade. He was just too much trouble. The answer to his truancy was to send him to boarding school far enough away from his own neighbourhood that he would be unable to escape. So the school suggested transferring Carlos to the Vocational Arts School in Santa Clara, a town situated in central Cuba, and eighty-five miles from home. Pedro and his reluctant son set out on what turned out to be a long seven-hour journey. It was not a happy father-son bonding time. They made many mistakes in their itinerary before they finally reached the school doors. Tired and relieved to have arrived at their destination at last, they were shocked when they were told that they had made their journey in vain. Not only was there no Grade IV boys' class, but the Santa Clara school only had a programme for prospective teachers of dance, not students. What's more, its staff had never received any communication from the Alejo Carpentier Provincial School of Ballet about a certain Carlos Junior Acosta Quesada. While Pedro was shattered physically and mentally by the news, the young boy's heart secretly soared with the hopes of, at last, being set free from his father's dreams. But as they were turned away, already other plans for his future were being developed. Pedro was told that the town of Pinar del Río in the south had a school where ballet was taught. 'They said they weren't sure that I would get in,' said Carlos, 'but my father was determined to try. It was by now too late to get home after our meeting so we had to stay overnight in Santa Clara – in the station.' Very early the next morning, the two of them caught the milk train back to Havana and told the family what had happened. Mustering up all his strength, the exhausted sixty-six-year-old Pedro got up at four o'clock the very next morning, and set off again. 'This time my father left me at home while he went off by bus alone to Pinar del Río – it was his home town – to try for a place at this other Vocational Arts School.' Again the headmistress was not over-enthusiastic about admitting Carlos – it seemed obvious that his reputation had reached her ears. 'Apparently my father started pleading with her, showing her my exam results, and begging her to give me the opportunity to continue my studies,' he said grimacing. Somewhat taken aback by the grown man's entreaties, she relented and it was agreed that Carlos could attend. 'I was on trial for a month so I knew that I had no choice but to stay there and work.' The threatening look from his father when he left was enough to tell Carlos that he had better mend his ways and knuckle down to work this time – or else.

Pinar del Río is 108 miles from Havana and a long bus or train ride, so, not having any regular pocket money, there was no way Carlos was able to escape school to return home and be enticed by football and breakdancing with his wayward friends. He boarded at the school during the week but at weekends, when the boarding department closed and students went home to their families, he had to stay with an older half-brother Pedro, one of his father's eight children from an earlier marriage whom he had never met until then. Here in a hovel of a home with a leaking roof, armies of cockroaches, and strained atmosphere, he tried to unwind from his hard week in school, feeling unwelcome and like an intruder who had to be suffered. Regularly, he had to endure the tempestuous physical and verbal battles between his half-brother and his wife, and when the atmosphere got too inflamed, he was delegated to an even worse shack at the end of the garden until peace reigned once more. There he would battle with legions of creepy crawlies, foul smells from the nearby river and the torrential downpours that came straight through the roof and soaked him as he lay in bed. He was often ill and feverish when he returned to school. Loneliness and self-pity soon took over and he longed for affection. 'Wednesdays were especially hard as they were the visiting days,' he recalled. 'Families would come to see the other kids, bringing special treats, and soon all the rooms were filled with laughter. But I had no one.' Carlos would skulk off feeling unloved and unwanted. He longed to see his mother again, to hear news of his family and he felt abandoned so far from home.

The school was well organised with good facilities and had a high reputation as a training ground for teaching the variety of classical arts it offered. 'When I started out, the government was paying for everything, so money to train in these different arts was not an issue. There was a collection of young people around me who really wanted to become ballet dancers. They saw ballet as being cool and of promising a good life. But this was certainly not my kind of "cool"', he remarked years later, laughing. He remained apathetic in his approach, going through the boring rituals each day without making any real effort. However, it was here at this school in Pinar del Río, at the age of thirteen, that he had his 'road to Damascus' revelation about ballet.

Sport was still uppermost in the young student's mind and on this occasion, as related in his book,* Carlos and several classmates had planned all week to watch a baseball game between the Havana home team he supported and the local Pinar del Río line-up, which everyone else in school supported. There was a lot of banter amongst them and Carlos prayed that the result would show that his home team was best and thus hopefully he would then gain some credibility

---

No Way Home, p.83

with his classmates. It was to be a good evening, and the day didn't go fast enough for the boys. Then, at the end of classes, the students were told that everyone was expected to go into town, to the local theatre that very night to watch a performance by the Ballet Nacional de Cuba that was touring around the country. Sport versus ballet – how could anyone compare the two? The boys all groaned and especially Carlos. But he had learned enough from past experiences to know that he had to be obedient to such orders from the school principal. Not in the cheeriest of moods, he set off with the other pupils to the theatre, only to find that he was sitting next to one of his teachers. Now he had no chance to sneak out. He would have to stay and feign interest. But nothing could stop him dreaming – how was the game going? Who was winning? The lights dimmed, the curtains opened and he tried to pull himself out of his reveries as some soft sylphs in flimsy tarlatans drifted across the stage. It was not the most persuasive sight for a reluctant young boy who would much rather have been cheering on his baseball team! Then suddenly he sat bolt upright. A male dancer had appeared – Alberto Terrero, one of the company's principals. He moved with astonishing grace and agility before suddenly leaping into the air, where, to Carlos' young incredulous eyes, he seemed to hover for an eternity before landing. The boy had never seen a man do that before. There was no one in the school who could move like that and this was the first time that Carlos had attended a ballet performance and seen men dance. At first he was convinced that a wire must have suspended him, but after scouring the stage with his eyes for proof, he soon realised that it was the man's technique that had sent him soaring. He was awestruck and decided there and then that he must do likewise. This is what he wanted to learn to do, no matter how hard it was to perform and no matter how long it took him. This, he resolved, is how my father must have imagined I would dance. He could hardly wait until class the next day. Once in the studio, not reacting to the taunts from the other boys because his baseball team sadly had lost the game, he renewed his energies into achieving. He had had his epiphanous moment and his life was transformed. Ballet now had a meaning for him and he wanted for the first time in his short life to succeed as a dancer.

Carlos now spent every moment he could in the studio practising steps over and over to strengthen his muscles. His teacher Juan Carlos González whom, in the past, Carlos had thought too disciplined and unfair, was amazed at this turnabout in his pupil, and the results that were being seen. He could see the fervour with which Carlos now attacked his work and that made him take much more interest in teaching him. Suddenly all of the young boy's passions seemed to be spent in the studio, practising, practising, practising. Well, almost all of them.

At thirteen, Carlos was maturing both physically and artistically and suddenly became interested in the opposite sex. This was an exciting discovery for him and, being vulnerable, he was quick to fall in love. But it seemed that each time he did, he would find that 'his' girl would go off with someone else, and down he'd sink in self-pity. Once again, he felt that it must be his lowly status that turned them away, his lack of material possessions, of being just a poor boy from the slums of Havana. So he turned to petty crime, stealing things from the other students in order to impress and to feel that he had worth. Of course he was caught and reprimanded not just in front of the ballet section, but of the whole school. Once again, the threat of suspension hung heavily on him and especially the fear of what his father would do to him if he were sent home in disgrace. Fortunately he now had supportive teachers who could see his new budding talent and interest, especially since his progress and determination were propelling him to achieve. They didn't want to lose him and wisely, instead of enforcing some dire punishment, they gave him responsibilities to keep him focused. He was chosen to perform principal roles in school productions and was regularly praised, which resulted in his getting good marks in exams. This upturn in his life should have raised his self-esteem. But it didn't. While he enjoyed showing off his newfound dancing skills in the studios, inside he loathed himself, his deceit, his lack of finesse and the petty crimes he had committed. These self-critical feelings trawled the rock bottom of his despair, yet they were not in vain. Carlos had no idea then, that later in his career as a principal dancer, he would be drawing on all these first-hand emotions, pulling them up from their submersed depths to bring them to amazing life in the challenging character roles he would be given, where they would add dramatic uniqueness to his technical abilities.

At last the course was over. The final exams were to be held back in Havana at his old school and in front of familiar teachers. It had been a long two years for Carlos away from home and family. Very occasionally, a kind teacher had given him his fare home for the weekend, but now he was returning for good to his own neighbourhood and to his mother. His maturing physique and his broken voice surprised her and his sisters kidded him. 'If they think I now look different then hopefully my old teachers won't recognise me,' he reasoned when he set off once more for L and 19 Streets to take the examinations that were to determine the next part of his training. It felt strange to re-enter the studio where it had all begun – the half-broken mirror was still there, the *barre* and the greasy marks on the wall around it, the rough wood floor filled with splinters that had ripped his ballet shoes to shreds. And those familiar faces – they were all sitting there in judgement, remembering, he was sure, the trouble he had caused. Teachers from all the regions and from Carlos' earlier classes at the school had come to watch the all-important examination class, and Carlos was determined to show them what he had learned and how he had improved and changed. He suddenly had a great desire to dance – and it showed. At the centre of the examining table was a small lady. This was the respected teacher named Ramona de Saá, who was known to her friends as Chery. She had noted Carlos when she had visited the school in Pinar del Río and now watched the proceedings that examination day, witnessing his potential and progress, as did other amazed teachers who remembered his inglorious history. An hour later, it was announced that a record-breaking ten students had passed, with Carlos receiving the highest score, an incomparable achievement. This meant that he was accepted back into the system and would now go to the National School of the Arts in Havana for his final two years of training. Here, Madame de Saá, who would be his teacher, was determined to prove that this young boy had a unique talent that needed to be carefully guided and developed correctly.

And she was so right. Her vision, conviction and deep love was to mould Carlos Junior Acosta Quesada from an insecure boy into the star he has become today.

4

The Realisation of His Potential – and Its Rewards

'Dance comes naturally to the Cuban people – but not perhaps ballet'

BY 1989, SIXTEEN-YEAR-OLD JUNIOR ACOSTA at last settled down into the daily life of a ballet student. He was now attending the National School of the Arts in a plush area north of Havana called Miramar. Just a few blocks from the turquoise waters of the Caribbean Sea, the school, airy and grand, is situated in the same area as the foreign embassies. Rather than face the long, time-consuming, crowded bus rides to and from home each day, Carlos opted to board at the school and found the experience a vast contrast to the accommodation he had had in Pinar del Río with its bugs, smells and leaky roofs. He got fed well and it was a pleasant place to live and after all, as he said, 'the state picked up all the costs'. The school building was surrounded by every kind of fruit tree – and yes, the temptation to shimmy up the trunk and help himself, as in his childhood, was still present and occasionally yielded to. But now he didn't get caught. Here, in this lovely environment, the young dancers had academic lessons together with the other arts students, studying Cuban culture, history, art, music, politics and languages – but to Carlos' relief, not subjects like mathematics and physics. When it came to their dance lessons, the students had to be bussed down into the heart of Havana for their daily ballet routines and repertoire classes where the contrast in facilities could not have been greater to those in Miramar. The cleanliness and spaciousness of the National School of the Arts building was exchanged for the oppressive crowded studios backstage at the Gran Teatro de la Habana. Standing in the Paseo del Prado, this baroque performing home of the Ballet Nacional de Cuba was built in 1837. Its marble entrance and staircase lead to the vast auditorium that seats 1,500, and oozes, if somewhat tattered today, old-world splendour and atmosphere. Yet backstage, its various studios are dark and airless and it is home to an assortment of feral cats (one of whom famously, during one ballet festival, paraded nonchalantly on stage in the middle of a performance of *Swan Lake*. It stopped to admire the scene before making an elegant exit, padding up the ersatz staircase with tail held high). Carlos and his fellow ballet students had to share the three studios with other dance students whose flamenco training, with all its stamping, hand-clapping, guitar music and singing, regularly overpowered the ballet pianist's rhythms, making it hard to concentrate. The uneven wooden floors were so rough and splintery that they snagged the students' canvas ballet shoes immediately, just as they had done in their earlier schools – and there were no replacements. There was only cold water in the showers – when they worked – and certainly no air conditioning in the muggy stifling temperatures. But in the studios, there was a great sense of happy dedication from all the dancers. The hardships and challenges they faced daily were eclipsed by their love of learning, and invoked their determination and will to succeed. Today, with government funding, the National School of Ballet has transferred to the centre of the capital where its headquarters are now an old, very beautiful renovated mansion, modelled on the Vendramin Calergi Palace in Venice, which had once been a private club for well-to-do businessmen. The contrasts to Carlos' own school experiences could not have been greater. Pristine and sparkling in white and gold, its double marble staircase with wrought-iron balustrades leads the way to the twenty-two studios and seven classrooms set over three floors. The students of today find themselves working in large, air-conditioned studios with wall-length mirrors on three sides. The high-ceilinged rooms are full of light and space, the envy of any ballet school worldwide. There is a physiotherapy department for massages, acupuncture, ultrasound and electrodes and a music room where the students can compile dance tapes.

The school day begins at eight thirty with the morning ballet class for all ages. Then there are *pointe* classes and, from age fourteen to fifteen upwards, *pas de deux* and repertoire classes. After lunch there are regular scholastic lessons of language, literature, aesthetics and history. The students are tested regularly and they have performances every two months, which give them practice and confidence for their future lives on stage. The atmosphere for today's young dance students is sheer luxury compared to when Carlos and his contemporaries were training.

On the academic curriculum both then and today, is a course that teaches of Cuba's roots in the world of classical ballet, and how and why this small country has become so highly regarded for this art at home and abroad. The answer to this is the work and dedication of one specific individual, Alicia Alonso, an iconic figure on a par with royalty in this communist country. The 'living legend' as she is known, has been responsible for establishing and maintaining the high standards of classical ballet in Cuba for over half a century. Born in Havana in 1920, young Alicia studied ballet with Nikolai Yavorsky, a Russian émigré, before setting off for New York in 1937 to appear on Broadway in musicals with her first husband, Fernando Alonso, whom she had married at the age of sixteen. In 1938, she made her debut on the American stage in a musical called *Great Lady* while still continuing her ballet studies. Proving herself to be a 'ballerina extraordinaire', she left the musical stage to join Lincoln Kirstein's Ballet Caravan (1939), then a year later Ballet Theatre (today's American Ballet Theatre), where she danced the works of many of the early twentieth century's great choreographers – Fokine, Massine, Tudor, Balanchine and de Mille. Her experiences with this vast palate of multi-faceted creations gave her rich credentials for the time when she would run her own company. In the next eight years, she performed both in Havana with Sociedad Pro-Arte Musical, and in America with Ballet Theatre, before returning home permanently with Fernando to set up the highly acclaimed Ballet Alicia Alonso in 1948, thus putting Cuba firmly on the world's artistic map.

President Castro's cultural aims for his people were to make culture free for everyone, and to find and develop talent throughout the country. So, given the high international reputation of the Alonsos, he approached them with the prospect of establishing first-rate classical ballet in Cuba. They proceeded to outline a nationwide plan to introduce dance to the masses, which received the president's blessing and, more essentially, financial support. They were given $200,000 to lay the foundations for a national company and for a school that would feed the company with future dancers. Over the past fifty years, both of these projects have received home and global recognition for the brilliant, versatile dancers that the system has produced. Classical ballet in Cuba is seen as one of the country's most highly esteemed 'exports' – along with cigars and tourism – bringing fame and pride to its people. Madame Alonso has held the position of artistic director of the ballet company since its inception, with Fernando Alonso as general director until 1974. She has also been its chief choreographer and as *prima ballerina assoluta*, she continued to dance well into her seventies despite near blindness due to detached retinas, a tragic disability which, since the 1940s, seriously dogged – but never permanently halted – her career. 'I have a passion for dance. It is my whole life,' she said. 'Nothing has stopped me from fulfilling my dreams.'* Two years after setting

---

* *Dance Now,* Vol 16: No 1, Spring 2007

up the company, the couple established the Provincial Ballet School of Havana and, later the National School of Ballet – hothouses of artistry where future stars have been, and continue to be, carefully preened and cultivated in the difficult disciplines of classical ballet. Fernando Alonso was the director from 1962–68 and has continued his involvement in its activities well into his nineties.

But the Alonsos' strategy reached further than the country's capital. The opportunity to study ballet was not just for those who lived in Havana. In realising Castro's goal of giving opportunities to every Cuban, the Alonsos proposed a countrywide search for talented youngsters who could train as dancers in local schools, which they would set up in the art-for-all project. The idea was approved and so annually they and their teachers set off to scour the countryside to find children with aptitude to teach, with the criteria that prospective students should have musicality, good body proportions and the ability to follow simple steps and rhythms. They travelled to all fourteen provinces, often in way-out bucolic and very poor parts of the island in their search. The system remains the same today as on those first journeys and selected youngsters now attend local elementary ballet schools. Because of the opportunities that a dance career offers, boys are encouraged to audition for ballet schools as much as girls. Unlike some

Western societies, here on this beautiful island, ballet dancing is seen as macho, not effeminate – though the young Carlos might not have readily agreed, remembering the flak he received from his hip-hop friends. Dancing is very much a part of the evolution of the Cubans' cultural heritage. Their ancestors from Africa and Spain mixed with Caribbean blood to create a unique concoction of passion, exuberance and vitality in natural body movements. Just stand on any street in Cuba and watch how people of every age walk – the hips sway, the upper body responds and the hands gesticulate expressively. Their animated conversations, lively eyes and whole bodies seem to be moving to some silent musical beat. It would seem that dance comes naturally to the Cuban people as something lived, not learned. But perhaps not ballet!

At the end of their early training in their local schools, the young dance students take exams and the most talented are then accepted into the two serious ballet schools in Havana or Camagüey. Today the students who are fortunate enough to get a place in the beautiful new National School of Ballet building train with a teaching staff comprised of dedicated ex-dancers who pass on their own knowledge gained through years of performing. The curriculum they teach – which includes folkloric and dance histories, French language and theatre studies, along with practical classes of a ballet technique created from a confluence of Italian, Russian, French and English styles with its unique Cuban-style blending – was devised by the director of the school, Ramona de Saá, and her team of staunch teachers. The small lady, her hair scraped back save for two trademark ringlets which she constantly twiddles, has guided the careers of most of the brilliant dancers in the Ballet Nacional de Cuba. She continuously turns out versatile, well-rounded performers from her school, dancers whose fastidious technique, bravura and brilliance would enhance any top-class company.

Like a fabled fairy godmother, she played the most significant role in the career of the student Carlos, especially in the second chapter of his life. Her love, vision and dogged devotion to instilling in him, not only the highest teaching, but also the motherly affection and security he so badly needed, gave Carlos the impetus to stay the course. 'Ramona is a second mother to me,' he says. 'She was the one that really formed me, educated me and prepared me for the competitions of Lausanne and Paris. She placed tremendous confidence in me. Together, we have lived through many stages of my life and both the good and bad things that have happened. You always need someone to help you, give you a hand. Whatever talent I have is due to her. I lived in very, very, very poor times and my neighbourhood was not the best. Sometimes I think what might have become of my life if she had not rescued me.'

Ramona de Saá and her identical twin sister Margarita started ballet classes with the Alonsos and later joined Ballet Alicia Alonso before both becoming teachers. Ramona de Saá is highly respected in ballet circles and often appears as a member of the jury on prestigious international ballet competitions. She takes great pride in all her students and their development – but none greater than with Carlos, whose lofty leaping figure in Houston Ballet's production of *Don Quixote* is present in a huge framed poster in her office opposite her desk.

Carlos took his time to be pulled into shape, but urged on with this love and interest in him, he pulled out all stops, determined to prove his ability and power as a dancer. One of the challenges he faced during his training and the country's hard economic times was the lack of energy food. Too often, he was unable to fulfil his potential in rehearsals due to hunger. Teachers would bring him bread and food from their own homes and Madame de Saá was one of those. 'That is another reason why our bond is so strong,' he acknowledges gratefully. At sixteen, he started to prove that his dancing ability was exceptional. He entered the Festival of Dance competition in Havana and won the gold medal and the first prize for a male dancer in the *Competencia Juvenil de Danza,* and was included on a school cultural exchange to Mexico where he had his first taste of the outside world. 'We were in Mexico City for two weeks,' he said. 'I was amazed to see so many people in their own cars, and people walking around wearing funny-looking sneakers – we had old-fashioned flat rubber ones. I cried when we all had to leave. I knew from that time that I had to travel.' An idea, so he thought, that was just a dream. He returned to school and worked hard, pushed on by an inner force.

For Cubans, the opportunity to travel abroad has normally been just a pipe dream. As in the former Soviet Union, the borders were, and still are, shut to all but a privileged few, especially since the plane ticket has to be paid for in foreign currency and its exorbitant price is beyond most people's means. It takes many weeks of paperwork to obtain a visa for cultural exchanges, and permission is normally only granted to be absent for a minimum of time, so there is rarely a possibility of staying to work abroad. At the ballet studios in Havana, Viengsay Valdés, today's prima ballerina of Ballet Nacional de Cuba, spoke of her dreams of working in another country, 'but only for an extended visit,' adding, 'and, if I could get a proper visa. There is so much that I want to dance, for example, ballets by MacMillan, especially his

Manon.'* At the moment, she is only able to get visas for cultural exchanges when invited for appearances at galas and festivals. Viengsay is a naturally brilliant dancer, effervescent in style as well as character and she has the amazing ability to stay on *pointe* and balance on one leg without wobbling for a full minute – 'My friend timed me in the studio,' she said laughing. The average length for most ballerinas is just a few seconds and it's Viengsay's poise, strength and exuberance, which keep her rock steady. Though technically unmusical and occasionally irritating to purist classicists, the 'trick' always brings the crowds, especially in Cuba, to their feet cheering as they love her sense of fun and daring. She regularly partners Carlos at festivals and special performances and their combined magnetic powers on stage are electrifying. But there was the odd occasion when their performances faced challenges. In 2006, the two were dancing the *Diana and Actaeon pas de deux* – a showy piece that bursts with technical wizardry – when Viengsay suffered an asthma attack in her solo. She slowed down in her leaps around the stage, coming almost to a halt, at which point Carlos flew in from the wings, in character, scooped her up and continued with her in his arms until the end of the music. It was a true moment of partnership. Later Viengsay said that although

---

* *Dance Magazine*, April 2009

she had felt unwell that evening, she was *not* going to miss the opportunity to dance with Carlos. 'I told the doctor to give me something to make me better – for just seven minutes of strength. But onstage I ran out of breath.'* Later, in talking about Carlos' career, Viengsay vigorously states that she would not like the long-term separation from her homeland such as he has had. 'I am happy when I get invited to dance on short visits abroad but I have my family here and we all get together each Sunday to play dominoes and talk. I would miss that.'

For Loipa Aranjo, one of Cuba's great ballerinas and respected teachers, there is a different emotion when one of her dancers leaves to go abroad. 'It's like a mother losing her child when you've been their teacher,' she says. 'A whole generation has grown up here with the political situation regarding the US restrictions imposed on travel. But the ban doesn't serve Cuba, the US people, culture or science. And why do they never point at other countries with problems – just to us, and our regime? They make it difficult for Cubans to travel to the US for work purposes and for our aspiring dancers to compete for example, in the international ballet competition at Jackson, Mississippi. It's such a shame for our talented young people to miss out. And it cuts in another way also

---

* *Dance Magazine*, April 2009

– little overseas trade means that we don't have the money for foreign choreographers to come and stage new works for us. Yes, we have lost many dancers to the West, but young Carlos never lost contact with us – he always came back for coaching and correcting.'

Sixty years of US embargo has left the island in a state of limbo, cut off from the world economically and culturally, which has certainly stifled opportunities for budding young dancers. But just occasionally, pockets in the system would arise when travel was permitted and Carlos was the right age at the right time. Suddenly the impossible was happening. He was given the greatest gift imaginable – Madame de Saá chose him and another student, Ariel Serrano, to accompany her to Italy to take part in a cultural exchange with the Teatro Nuovo di Torino during their penultimate year of training. For Carlos, this was another great turning point in his life. The unique talent that he had been developing would no longer be seen only inside Cuba, but would soon be stepping out on the path of international status and acclaim.

A year in Italy was beyond the wildest dreams of any sixteen-year-old boy, let alone one from the *barrio*. Impatiently wanting to set off and start their new adventure, the boys prepared for their government-approved departure. They were given permission and money to buy some respectable clothing at the special state store to better represent their country outside in the West. And they were drilled on how to behave and be a credit to their country. The day for their departure arrived and their excitement mounted. But as time passed, their anticipated visas didn't materialise. They waited all day and, as the plane's departure time approached, then passed, their hopes were dashed. Perhaps it had all been a wind-up, a payback for the nuisance he had caused, and there was no trip, Carlos pondered anxiously. Perhaps they wouldn't be able to go after all. Severely disappointed, Carlos went home to his family and settled down dejectedly in front of the TV set. To his horror, he saw a report of a plane crash just outside Havana's José Martí airport, which had killed over 100 people. The high winds of the day had turned into a cyclone and the plane had been caught up in it. The Acosta family sat glued to the screen in disbelief as they watched the terrible aftermath of the crash. The plane had been bound for Italy. Had the visas come through in time, both Carlos and Ariel would have been on it. Their relief for their son's safety was enormous and that night, Pedro gave his saints some extra titbits in gratitude. Finally, a week later, with the precious visas in hand, the two boys, highly excited but also saddened at leaving their families, set off for their new venture.

5

The Italian Job and
European Acclaim

'The Cuban won the competition'

IMAGINE WAKING UP IN A FREE COUNTRY for the first time – especially when you are a teenager and come from the slums of Los Pinos – and then realising that you are going to live in this freedom for a whole year. The young boys couldn't believe their eyes at what was accepted as normal living to the Italians, especially the vast quantities of food available each and every day. They also marvelled at the cafes spilling onto the streets, filled with the natural joy and laughter of people who didn't have to spend all their days in queues searching for basic food. To the boys, it seemed that everywhere in this affluent society, the abundance of luxury was visible and flaunted, though their own accommodation was more what they were used to. Madame de Saá had flown ahead and had found a very small apartment for the three of them to share with Nancy Fresneda, a Cuban ballet teacher. There was one bedroom with two beds and a pull-out couch in the living room that the boys shared. The intimacy reminded him of his own home. It was an arrangement however that didn't last long. Carlos and Ariel, whose late-night salsa talents were greatly admired at the clubs they frequented, quickly found girlfriends and the two boys moved elsewhere.

The small company of Turin's Teatro Nuevo consisted of ten women and five men, so the two extra males were warmly welcomed into the studios that first morning, though Carlos felt sure that the stares, albeit subtle ones, from the other dancers, were because of his skin colour. Chery, as Carlos, away from the formalities of his Cuban ballet school, now called Madame de Saá, gave class and oversaw her two wards' rehearsals. There was so much to learn, and learn fast, as the company soon set off on tour to such historic Italian towns as Bergamo and Venice, where, at the tender age of sixteen, Carlos partnered the leading ballerina Luciana Savignano. His performing was spotted in all the towns they visited and the press called him a natural born talent, admiring his ability to show fine virtuoso technique. Carlos was a happy boy, progressing well and quickly adapting to the routine of company life in this exciting environment. Still unaware of his burgeoning talent, he was amazed when one day Chery suggested that he should enter for the prestigious International Prix de Lausanne competition in Switzerland. It is an event that most young dancers dream of participating in, and where many stars of the future have first been spotted. Chery was convinced that it was his time to shine and that he would do well. 'I had trained him over the years and we had a lot of support from the Teatro Nuovo di Torino, which financed us economically,' she recalled. 'Now everyone said to me: "Why don't you send him to Lausanne, he surely must win! And from Italy, Lausanne is so near!"'

The Prix de Lausanne, the most prestigious of youth ballet competitions, is an annual event founded in 1973 by Philippe and Elvire Braunschweig for talented young students between fifteen and eighteen years of age. Lasting one week, the competition is held in snowy January on the raked stage of the Théâtre de Beaulieu in the beautiful Swiss town of Lausanne, and has become the Mecca for dedicated ballet students. While the standard is extremely high, the rewards are great, and not just monetary. The best of the young contestants receive either cash prizes or scholarships to top-name ballet establishments in many countries – and for those coming from small schools in distant lands, it is a dream to win the opportunity to continue training at one of these. The top prize of the competition, though not always presented, is the gold medal. Being named a winner at the Prix de Lausanne opens doors for dancers throughout their careers, and for nearly forty years, the internationally acclaimed competition has seen its many prize-winners become stars in their own right – globally renowned dancers such as Italian Alessandra Ferri, British Darcey Bussell, Japanese Tetsuya Kumakawa, Romanian Alina Cojocaru, Russian Diana Vishneva.

The very thought of the numerous possibilities that could come from such a competition gave Carlos impetus. He had been in Italy for several months now and still missed his family with whom he had no contact. He was also suffering from an unhappy schoolboy love affair with an older Italian dancer, so now decided to put all his passion and drive into perfecting his technique. Chery guided him in all his rehearsals, cleansing any minute fault and stopping him from his exertions when he doggedly continued long after the workday had elapsed. Finally he had found the fire in his soul that propelled him onwards. Ballet had become an addiction and all his energies were thrust into it.

His Cuban passport naturally caused problems in obtaining a visa for Switzerland and once again his patience and trust were sorely tested as complications and delays arose. Finally, on the day before the last possible date of departure dawned, the visa arrived. Carlos' application had been accepted and he received his number for the competition: 127 – the very last competitor. He could now set off to show his finest style to those who mattered in international ballet circles. In January 1990, with good wishes winging him on from his company friends, he flew off to another European country and to, hopefully, one step higher on the ladder of an incredible future. His teacher and mentor, Chery, was needed in Turin to help stage new productions, so she assigned a Cuban called Raoul to accompany Carlos. He turned out to be a lacklustre character who was of little help. Though purportedly able to speak five languages, Carlos quickly discovered that these so-called skills were very poor except when it came to flirting with the girls.

The young dancer tried hard not to let anything affect him, but as before, when mixing with other young people of his own age, his confidence took a beating. The other boys looked so neat, were mostly fine-boned and princely in bearing. He was muscular, dark-skinned and sported a rather abundant Afro hairstyle. Being without an advisor or coach for those final moments after months of daily rehearsals put pressure on him – and Raoul was no help in relaying the nitty-gritty details of the organisation. Carlos badly wanted to win for Chery and for his family, but he also shouldered the burden of knowing that he had to win for Cuba – coming second wasn't an option as far as the government was concerned. 'The competition was harder and closer than it is today,' Chery remembered. 'Coaches weren't supposed to make contact with their students, though there were many there advising them. I only attended the last round and when I arrived at the theatre, I saw Carlos training with the others. But instead of the black and white regulation outfit that the boys had to wear, he was wearing red! He stood out and I was afraid that it wasn't going to be good for his evaluation.' Fortunately, it didn't affect the final result.

The competition started with daily class on stage with everyone wearing his number on his front and back and those selected to continue were given the chance to show off their dances wearing their practice clothes. Carlos had worked hard on his solo from the ballet *Don Quixote* and now it came alive with joy and exuberance. He felt that he had found the secret of performance – and it was not just in dancing technically correct steps, or leaping very high or going fast. He realised that dancing must be done with love and expression that came from deep within one's soul. His performance was impressive and magnetic and despite the rule that no one should applaud the competitors, the hall erupted with clapping. His contemporary solo called *Tocororo* and choreographed by Carla Perotti, also showed off his athleticism and supple virtuosity. He flew through the air, bare-chested in brown patterned tights with his hands flexed. His dancing was light but his gestures strong. His natural ability to fly and turn made his audience catch their breath. Suddenly everyone wanted to know him and be his friend. He easily sailed through to the semi-final.

The following day he arrived early at the theatre and quickly put on his costume and make-up, excited about performing again. As always, he was last on the list to perform, so he decided to go down to the wings and watch the other competitors. It was a bad mistake and one that he would not have made had Chery been with him. She would have made sure that he remained alone, focusing on his solo and convincing him that he could do it, that he could win. But all that was well and truly forgotten when he watched one after another of the excellent young dancers showing off his or her skills. He grew nervous, his confidence clunked to the lowest rung. By the time it was his turn, his dancing and mental state were affected. He couldn't attain the height he normally did and lost his balance. He couldn't put emotion into his steps. He knew he had danced badly and feared that he had let everyone down, including himself. As the judges deliberated, he went off to dinner in a very depressed mood with a less than compassionate Raoul, and reluctantly returned to the theatre to await the results. It seemed pointless to Carlos to stand in line with the others, waiting as the successful numbers were read out. But at the very end of a list of those competitors who had successfully made it into the final round, he suddenly heard number 127, his number, called, and the astonished boy thanked the saints for giving him another chance. He was determined not to let this next opportunity to achieve be thwarted. He celebrated his success by immediately returning to the hotel and going to bed early.

There were eleven finalists and all of them excellent dancers-in-the-making. Having learned his lesson from the day before, Carlos took great care this time to concentrate on his performance, getting warmed up gently and thoroughly and not being distracted by what was going on around him. He realised that his next performance could and would change his life forever – and he had to succeed. Once more he was dancing the solo from *Don Quixote* but this time he was confident and ready. He went on stage, cued the music and set off, simply flying across the stage defying gravity while showing his musicality and control. It was a stunning performance and he felt positive about his dancing. He had danced as he knew he could, technically secure and artistically exciting, and as he took his bow at the end, the hall exploded with cheering and flashing cameras.

The famed American dance critic of the *New York Times*, Anna Kisselgoff, who was in the audience, reported of seeing the young Cuban boy for the first time: 'Mr Acosta's bravura in an extract from *Don Quixote* rendered with his typical joyfulness, provoked an ovation even at the semi-finals.'* She would write years later after seeing him perform professionally in a gala in New York City: 'The exuberance and phenomenal technique he showed at the Prix de Lausanne competition several years ago are still there. But now there are also nobility and elegance.'†

Carlos was thrilled and appreciative that the audience recognised his talent. Feeling so good inside himself, he finally realised that he had escaped from that poisoning fear of lack of self-worth. He had proved himself a dancer. The judges huddled, the audience chattered and finally the moment came for the results. Dancers were called one by one to the stage to receive their diplomas and awards but since it all was done in the French language, Carlos had no idea who had won what. He assumed he had not been chosen when he saw the boy whom he thought best in the competition go up to receive his award. It seemed to Carlos that all the prizes had been given out. There was a pause, then came an announcement

* *New York Times*, 29 January 1990
† *New York Times*, 9 September 1996

in French which Carlos didn't understand, followed by 'Carlos Acosta from Cuba' which he did recognise.* He was stunned and went up to receive his prize from the chairman, thanking him and bowing to the thunderous applause from the auditorium. He was happy to have received something, though he had no idea what it was that he had won until later when he took off the lid of the box. Then he saw that he had been awarded the highest prize, the coveted gold medal only awarded to truly exceptional dancers. He was thrilled to receive it but his greatest joy was that Chery and Nancy had been able to come to Switzerland to see the final round – and his huge success.

'He danced *Don Quixote* as his classical variation and *Tocororo* as his modern work in excellent form,' a very proud Chery said, remembering that special occasion. There was much jubilation when they went out to celebrate that evening and it was wonderful for Carlos to be able to share this excitement with them. 'The next morning all the newspapers were talking about his triumphs,' Chery recalled proudly. 'I phoned the Cuban Embassy but it was too early – there was no one at work – so I left a message on the answer machine: "The Cuban won the competition!" Before that incredible moment, I had told Carlos: "If

---

* *No Way Home*, p.132

you dance well, there will be no one on the jury who will vote against you." I had so much confidence in him and I always had such trust in him. He danced perfectly.'

Carlos' face was splashed over all the newspapers and he did many television interviews. Suddenly, he had become a celebrity among his colleagues and he wondered where his future would take him after he graduated. He spent a happy last few months in Turin before returning to Cuba. But there was one big question – was his freedom to travel and opportunity to show the world what he could do about to end? It was a worrying thought.

Arriving back at the airport in Havana, his school friends greeted him like a football hero and it was good to see them all again. 'Everyone was so proud of me. The school had organised a bus to bring them all out to the airport,' remembered Carlos, smiling. 'It was amazing. They all wanted to shake my hand and pat me on the back.' He hurried home to his family, a joyful reunion with his mother, and a handshake from his father. Carlos also found that in his absence that year, his sister Berthe had not only married but had found religion. She was devoted and determined to convert and influence her young brother. Back at ballet school and thus only home at weekends, Carlos found that he had to study the Bible to appease her passion whenever he came home. He didn't understand much but her zeal was overwhelming. As her obsession grew greater and greater, the family feared that she might end up with the same fate as Aunt Lucía. After several excruciatingly embarrassing episodes, Berthe was finally diagnosed as having paranoid schizophrenia. Back once more in boarding school, this affected Carlos' work and every waking thought. The wheel of self-condemnation and guilt started spinning again. Perhaps he could have prevented the situation from arising had he stayed at home with the family instead of travelling to Italy. Was he to blame for her illness? He had returned to school after Turin and Lausanne with renewed purpose and dreams, but now he was wracked with anxiety about his sister and he wanted to support her and his family by being at home and not away at school. Yet again he angered his father when, unable to sleep for mulling over the situation, he escaped the dormitory one night by climbing out of the second-floor window and down a tree. Arriving home so unexpectedly in the early hours of the morning, his father was furious and a great argument ensued in which Pedro told his son in no uncertain terms that, because he possessed this incredible and now recognised talent, his duty had to be to his art alone. He was to think of nothing else, to completely forget his family and its problems, and pursue only his career. Hearing this tirade yet again, Carlos retorted, shouting, as he raced away in fear of being hit, that he hated his father for his blinkered, strict views. The confrontation drew him down into greater depths, which he could not hide. His despondent attitude was noticed by Chery, who recognised that she had to do something to take his mind off a situation that was certainly not his fault. So she entered him into the prestigious Paris International Dance Competition, held biennially for the world's talented stars-in-the-making. It meant hard physical work that she hoped would keep him from ruminating over the family situation. And it did help. But this time there was a different challenge to surmount. How were they to find the money to pay for all the expenses such a trip would incur? Unable to find sponsorship from all the normal sources, Chery made a rash promise to someone that, if they would put up the money for the two of them to go to Paris, then she and Carlos would repay the loan with the prize money. Now there was real pressure on Carlos to win.

In late November 1990, Carlos set off for France, though still with a disturbed mind. His journey was very long, via Moscow where he had to stop overnight. 'I remember it being very cold – about minus twenty – and we were in this terrible hotel a long way out of the centre which must have had only half a star! Everything was so dirty and cold, and in the bathroom – no water came out of the taps as everything was frozen – there was just a terrible noise like the walls were coming down.' As well as suffering travel fatigue, he was still troubled about Berthe when he finally took to the stage. Yet, even with his lack of concentration and the fact that he and Chery hadn't been assigned a practice room and had had to rehearse in the Cuban Embassy's conference room, his problems dissolved as he danced passionately and fervently. Again he wowed the judges and audiences alike. In the heart of the French capital, he was presented with the Grand Prix de la Ville de Paris and gold medal, and also awarded the Frédéric Chopin Prize, by the Polish Artistic Corporation for his spectacular dancing. Tears, not of happiness for his success, but of release finally from all the sadness he had been harbouring, poured down his face. However, his great joy at that moment was the knowledge that Chery would be able to pay back the debt owed.

It was earlier in that November of 1990 that Carlos was spotted by foreign journalists at the biennial Festival Internacional de Ballet de la Habana. He was taking class given by Alicia and Fernando Alonso's daughter Laura. 'I remember, it was in the ballet studio behind the company building on 5th and E streets," Carlos recalled years later. The entrance was through a small insignificant doorway and up a crumbling staircase. There, in a dingy, darkened studio – either because of one of the many power cuts, or maybe just a way of keeping the oppressive temperature down – the class of young boys were going through their steps. All were very good, of a very high standard. But two stood out from the rest. One was a handsome, slim-built mulatto with twinkly eyes and a dazzling smile – his name, Jose Manuel Carreño. The other, a gangly but virile, dark-skinned, curly-haired boy whose wide smile showed a rather fetching gap in his front teeth, was Carlos. As he leapt across the floor, there was fire in his dancing and yet he made it all look so easy. The two teenagers competed against each other in a friendly match of 'who could do the most turns', 'jump the highest', 'spin the fastest'. They were amazing and their incredible energy was exhausting to watch – but so impressive.

Following his triumph in Paris, Chery took Carlos with her whenever she had teaching assignments in South America to give him opportunities to perform, and he benefited from her motherly concern and professional experience. As the new year dawned on Carlos' final months as a student, there was great excitement amongst the dancers of Ballet Nacional de Cuba when they heard that Ivan Nagy, the artistic director of English National Ballet, was coming to Cuba to audition dancers for his company – specifically, strong, black male dancers. The handsome Hungarian, who had been an elegant and graceful *danseur noble*, had partnered the brilliant Russian ballerina Natalia Makarova when she first defected from the Kirov Ballet to come to the West.

Though still a student, Carlos was encouraged by his teachers to apply. His audition was a pretty poor effort as he was given a partner he had never danced with before and they had had no time to practise. She knew one version, he another and they often found themselves going in different directions. However, Nagy saw only the potential of this talented young boy and immediately offered him a contract – as principal dancer. Wisely Chery asked for time to think – Carlos had still to graduate. But she carefully noted all the information about the job, saying she would keep in touch.

In June 1991, at just eighteen, the once reluctant dancer who certainly would have chosen a career as a footballer had he had his way, took his final exams and graduated from the National School of Ballet with the highest qualifications and a gold medal. He went on to win the Grand Prix in the third *Competencia Juvenil de Danza*, and in July, the gold medal in the Osimo competition in Italy.

It looked as though his father had been right all along.

6

Jeté-ing Off to London

'Showing the English public what he could do'

WHEN THE YOUNG BALLET STUDENTS took their final exams to graduate as professional dancers, they were all eager to know in which of Cuba's several companies each of them would be placed. The results came in and Carlos saw that his newfound dedication and conduct had been rewarded. Five men and two women were taken into the Ballet Nacional de Cuba – and Carlos was one of them. But he was bewildered. Just a short while ago he had been offered a position as principal dancer in one of Europe's great companies. Now he found that he had been seconded to the corps de ballet, albeit in Cuba's top ballet company. It did not take him long to work out what a long journey lay ahead to reach principal status here, as the company boasted many excellent male dancers. What hope and future would there be for him?

Added to this disappointment, Carlos realised that he would be losing Chery, his loyal and dedicated teacher, when he finally left school to join the company at the end of the summer. She had to remain with her new school pupils while he, as corps de ballet member, would no longer have that personal one-to-one coaching. Chery, however, had plans for one last trip during the summer break before the new season started when she would lose her exceptional student. She still had work to do in Turin, so she took Carlos with her to dance with the company again. Being back in a familiar setting with old friends who loved and appreciated him, and having the opportunity to show how well he now could dance, made Carlos happy. But he was in for a shock – a huge shock.

Invited over to Chery's apartment one evening after work, Carlos discovered that she had a surprise for him. She had made all the necessary plans for him to take up Ivan Nagy's offer of a principal dancer contract at English National Ballet, and that he was to be in London by the very next week. It was not a spur-of-the-moment idea that Chery had had – she had been thinking this over for some time especially when she found out through her ballet contacts what Carlos' debut with the Ballet Nacional was to be. The troupe was going on tour to Mexico and his name was down on the casting list of the beautiful two-act romantic ballet *Giselle*. But he was not going to be able to show off his special style in the production – he was to be one of the falconers in Act One. This role simply involved walking on stage in a procession that heralds the royal hunting party with a stuffed wooden bird on his arm. Chery had been horrified to see such a waste of talent, irrespective of the company's pecking order, and astutely realised that her favourite pupil had to leave Cuba if his exceptional talent was to progress and not stagnate. Knowing there would be recriminations for her part in his unauthorised departure, she was still willing to take the risk. Carlos' future was at stake. Fortunately for Chery, after the initial mutterings of what she had done had died down, her reputation and her many years of excellent hard work in the National School of Ballet were instrumental in restoring respect, and admiration. She has since been honoured for her devotion and dedication with the highest Cuban award – the Medal of Merit. And she has always kept in touch with Carlos wherever he has been. 'He always comes to my house and to the School every time he comes to Cuba,' adding sadly: 'When the first news came that my daughter had died in Mexico, Carlos was at his home here in Cuba. Since he had overseas contacts, he heard about it before me and immediately came to my house and broke the bad news to me. He still asks for my advice and normally he listens to me and does what I tell him to do.'

Chery still continues to nurture the great talent that evolves from the National School of Ballet in Havana. She has overseen the careers of many gifted young dancers, and in recent years, it has been that of Carlos' nephew Yonah, sister Marilin's son. A handsome young man with the family smile and sparkling eyes, and a leaner body than his uncle, Yonah exudes the Acosta fire and energy, and Chery's guidance has turned him into the beautiful and brilliant dancer he is today. His uncle's pride in him is well justified. At age thirteen, Yonah took on the role of the young Carlos in the semi-autobiographical work *Tocororo* that Carlos created in 2003 and showed poise and great stage presence as well as fantastic dancing ability even at that young age. Watching him in one of the school's spacious and bright studios back in Havana in 2008 felt like déjà-vu – of seeing Carlos as a student eighteen years earlier. This younger version of the great Cuban dancer, full of energy and confidence, shot around the studio in high, airborne *jetés* (where one leg is extended forward and the other backward, stretched out straight), and he finished with a pirouette that got faster and faster before he suddenly slowed it down to a perfectly balanced and accurate stop. He has his uncle's physical energy and talent to push the barriers of technique as far as possible and has fun in doing it.

Carlos smiles at the mention of his name, but adds, 'He has it too easy. He doesn't know what it is like to struggle like I did and how important it is for interpreting a role to feel those emotions. I buy him everything he needs and have helped him in many ways. Now it is up to him to succeed.' Yonah has successfully won prizes at various international ballet competitions, and back in Chery's office, hanging opposite Carlos' leaping poster is another equally large one of Yonah – 'her' two boys soaring as though to conquer the world. When she speaks of them, her striking eyes relay the pride and love she has for them both. But on that last day in Italy, when she bid farewell to an anxious Carlos at the Turin airport for his flight to London, those same bright blue eyes filled with tears. Her very special, much-loved young pupil was setting out on his own to show the world what unique talents he had to offer. He was no longer a boy – he had become a man.

Fortunately for the world of dance, the sun was shining on the day that Carlos arrived in London in 1991. If it had been dark and dank as it so often is, he may have jumped on the next plane home. But the fine weather gave him a good impression of the city sparkling in all its historic splendour. Carlos was taken to a hotel where he stayed for his first week, before moving into an apartment in Olympia, an area not far from the English National Ballet headquarters in Jay Mews, Kensington, with his good friend Jose Manuel Carreño and his wife Lourdes Novoa who were also dancing there.

Within weeks of joining the company, eighteen-year-old Carlos was chosen to represent English National Ballet at a gala concert to be staged at the Royal Opera House in Covent Garden, where many other famous international stars were also performing. Carlos was invited to dance the male solo from the ballet *Le Corsaire*, known for its flying leaps and stage-devouring *jetés*, and welcomed the opportunity, however nerve-wracking, to show London society what he could do. He had not heard of the other dancers who were also participating, names such as Darcey Bussell and Natalia Makarova, well known even outside the ballet circle. But he had heard of Diana, Princess of Wales, back home in Cuba, and whom he excitedly discovered would be at the gala and would come on stage to greet the dancers afterwards. It was not to be the only time that the two would meet. The Princess was Patron of English National Ballet and not only attended special performances of the company, boosting tickets sales through the publicity, but would slip in from her home at Kensington Palace across the street from the Jay Mews studios to watch the dancers in rehearsals. Being a lover of ballet all her life, she also took her own private classes there in a secluded studio, far from paparazzi eyes.

Carlos' remembrance of his first meeting with her on stage after the gala is etched in his memory – her natural friendliness, her pure white skin, her sparkling clear blue eyes which firmly focused on him as she said something to him – and of his being completely tongue-tied due to lack of the language. He wasn't any more loquacious when he met the Princess for the second time. He had just performed the Nutcracker prince and had returned to his dressing room where he had covered his face in cold cream and stripped out of his costume. 'I was sweaty and bare-chested,' he recalled, 'and there was this knock on the door. I thought it was someone from wardrobe for my costume and grabbed a towel. The door opened and there she stood, beaming her smile and congratulating me while I clutched my little towel and couldn't say a thing!'

Carlos proceeded to gain recognition in the many roles he was given to dance at English National Ballet. Whenever homesickness struck or the weather was awful, he would think of the stagnancy of what he would be doing in the company back home and knew that he was in his right place here in England, daily learning something new. He made his debut with the company in 1991 while on tour around England, as the great warrior and tribal leader in the Polovtsian Dances, the dancing interlude in Borodin's rousing opera *Prince Igor*. Here the general public had their first glimpse of the young Cuban man and his special brand of raw physicality and were thrilled by what they saw. He propelled himself with complete abandon around the stage in a frenzy of activity, whipping up the crowds both on and off stage with his animalistic, seemingly superhuman intensity. As the ballet ends, the warrior leader comes to the front of the stage and begins a series of never-ending whirling turns, which get faster and faster until the curtain falls. With his extraordinary technical abilities Carlos immediately made his mark on the incredulous British ballet audience, giddied by the speed and accuracy that he had demonstrated.

Christmas came and with it *The Nutcracker* – over and over again. As the main fund-raiser for their coffers, this well loved ballet is performed long before and during the holiday season in most classical ballet companies around the world. And English National Ballet was, and is, no exception. The company's two-act ballet, choreographed by Ben Stevenson, was a charming and popular production and part of the company's repertoire from the 1990s to the early 2000s. The British-born choreographer was renowned for breaking the mould of age-old traditions both in his own company, the Houston Ballet, and in the staging of his own works. Now in 1991, from all the excellent principal men at English

National Ballet, he chose Carlos to be the Prince for the opening of the London season – yes, the Prince, the very role Carlos thought he would never dance due to his colour. But after the initial surprise, he was happy to prove himself in the role, little realising that, in the not too distant future his life was going to be re-mapped by the very man whose steps he was dancing. Stevenson was to play a large and immensely important role in the young man's development, of both his dancing and his self-esteem.

Ben Stevenson had flown to London to rehearse his ballet in the studios of English National Ballet, and astonished Carlos when, at the end of the session, he casually invited him to dance with his company in America. Somewhat flustered, and convinced that he'd never get a visa, Carlos did not give the director a direct answer. Stevenson, assuming that Carlos' lack of response to his invitation was negative, left without further discussion and returned to Houston, leaving Carlos to mull over and regret not following up the idea.

Despite his initial lack of fluency in the language, Carlos fitted quickly into the daily routine of life in English National Ballet. He was given more and more opportunities to expand his technique, and director Nagy, renowned for his own refined dancing, gave him lessons in the finer methods of partnering. It was aesthetically acceptable to be an athlete and a firecracker performer some of the time, but Carlos also had to be taught the cultured demands of classical ballet. Used to being the powerhouse out in front, Carlos had to learn the delicate finesse of standing back and presenting his ballerina in the best way possible. He danced the pristine and technical *pas de deux* from *La Bayadère* with Lourdes, which demanded gentle and considerate attention to his ballerina before taking off in his own solos that enabled him to show off his exceptional abilities. His next partner was Maria Teresa del Real, a vivacious dancer from Spain who, like Carlos, enjoyed showing off the fireworks of *Don Quixote*. He was also given two legendary older and very experienced ballerinas to partner, which for a somewhat tentative eighteen-year-old was knee-knocking. The first, twenty-five years his senior, was the ethereal and seemingly fragile Eva Evdokimova, an international ballerina who was considered exceptional in the traditional romantic roles for her lightness and delicacy. She had been the favourite partner of the great Russian dancer, Rudolf Nureyev, in his later dancing years; now she was dancing with this young kid! However, their partnership was much admired – she gave him her experience and he brought his youthful vitality to her.

Carlos was also given one of the Bolshoi Ballet's most brilliant ballerinas to partner – Ludmila Semenyaka, who had so impressed British critics

with her delicate, filigree, yet sharply defined performances when she danced with the famed Russian
company on its tour to Britain in the 1980s. Now
aged thirty-nine, she had been invited to London to
perform as a principal guest ballerina with English
National Ballet. She had danced with many of the
experienced principal men in the company and now
she found she was to be partnered with the eighteen-
year-old Cuban boy.

'For someone of such a young age, I was enchanted
by his mastery of ballet,' she reminisced back home in
Moscow. 'He had a natural figure for a ballet dancer
and a reverence for art – I wanted him to reach the
heights. And he has. He possesses a gorgeous and tender heart, and his inner soul is evident in his dancing.' Even though Carlos had to bear the brunt of her
often sharp criticisms and demands when things got
tough during their rehearsals, and admits laughingly
that he was afraid of her – 'it was always my fault if it
went wrong'. Luda, as she is known, admired his dili-
gence to learn. 'He understood partnering very well
– he tried very hard – and he had enormous reverence for his partners.' Out of the studios and off stage,
she had a genuine, almost motherly affection and
admiration for him, even though communication
was very challenging with their paucity of English.
'I never thought of him as anything but a beautiful
dancer. He has reached the height of Cuban ballet in

the continuation of the ballet traditions that Alicia
Alonso established. Good for him, good for Cuba
and good for the world.'

As the year proceeded, Carlos found himself enjoy-
ing life with the company. But Stevenson's invitation
was often at the back of his mind, though he could
see no way of following that dream. Yet the seed of
possibility had been planted and Carlos found himself constantly thinking of the opportunity he surely
had missed. For him, the political situation between
his homeland and the USA was still volatile. With
no diplomatic relations between the two countries,
as a Cuban he could not see how he could possibly
work in America. His thoughts went back to his
extended family now in Miami, those who had set off
from Cuba to seek a new life when he was just a boy,
leaving him and his immediate family behind. Their
departure had left a huge indelible scar on him when
his relatives had refused to take him, his sister and
his father with them because of their colour. Due to
the political climate, there had been no contact with
them at all during those eleven years.

But that was to change. Soon after Stevenson's
departure, Carlos found himself at a 'Patrons of
English National Ballet' function, sitting next to an
American diplomat who handled Cuban-American
affairs. In their conversation together, Carlos poured
out his story to his interested dinner partner. Within

weeks, he was overjoyed to find that he had been granted a tourist visa to visit America, courtesy of the sympathetic diplomat. Soon Carlos was winging his way to Miami and a reunion with his grandmother, aunts and cousins, who had left him and his immediate family behind.

It was a memorable but unsettling week that Carlos spent with his relatives in a country that far exceeded his expectations for its easy, stress-free lifestyle and extravagant abundance of consumer goods. His aunt's home was spacious and modern and he thought of what his mother still had to put up with each day back in Los Pinos. Seeing him again for the first time in over a decade made his relatives uncomfortable and somewhat repentant for the treatment that they had inflicted on the family they had left behind in their homeland. The insensitive bias and fear that had divided the close-knit family obviously played on their emotions especially when Carlos organised a three-way telephone call to his mother via a friend in Canada. Tears poured down his grandmother's face as she talked to her daughter for the first time since she had left to live in this new world. Sadly they were never destined to meet again.

A week in Miami with his relations was sufficient and Carlos was happy to return to London and his newfound friends. But he was not to stay there for long. After a rehearsal one day, he fell badly on his ankle and was in much pain and unable to walk. An X-ray showed he had a bone spur that needed an operation and he found himself in hospital alone and unable to move. 'I realised that my visit to America had unsettled and troubled me and, on my return, I had not been able to concentrate, hence the fall,' he said. The days in hospital were very long and lonely and only broken up by visits from Lourdes who would tell him the latest gossip from the company. But the healing was a slow process. After eight long weeks and still in a lot of pain, he tried to dance again, feeing guilty that he was not fulfilling his contract. Since he was unable to jump, he was given roles that kept him more or less floor-bound. He tried his hardest to feel positive but deep down he knew that he could not remain a principal with English National Ballet while dancing so pathetically. He was also being challenged mentally. Spending so long alone with only his thoughts, he started having hallucinations and feared that he might be turning into a schizophrenic like his Bible-bashing sister Berthe.

He gave his initial London career one last huge effort when he stepped in at the last minute to replace another injured dancer in *Le Spectre de la Rose*. This celebrated one-act classical work, created by Michel Fokine, was made famous by the legendary Russian dancer Vaslav Nijinsky in 1911. Depicting the soul of a rose given to a dreamy young girl, it requires high leaps with non-stop dancing, all done with supreme lightness and, seemingly, lack of effort. Carlos dosed himself up with painkillers before stepping out – or rather, leaping onto – the stage, since the Rose's first entrance is through an open window. He performed the piece brilliantly with amazing grace and buoyancy. However, when the drugs wore off he was in such excruciating pain that he knew he could not proceed with his career any longer in such agony. He returned to the apartment, packed his bags with his few possessions and the gifts for his family he had bought during his time in London, and, the next day, set off to the airport for the flight home to Cuba for an operation – and to his mother's care.

7

Back Where He Started – and Beyond

'Nothing is impossible with the right lawyer'

ARRIVING BACK IN HIS OLD NEIGHBOURHOOD to the familiar street, its smells and noises, Carlos felt an inner joy and peace. He had been unable to warn his family that he was coming so when he turned up unannounced, they were obviously overjoyed and emotional at seeing him again, though saddened by his injury. Stuffing plates of his favourite food – black beans, rice, chicken, plantains – in front of him, they plied him with questions, wanting to hear all his tales of life in London, and especially of meeting Princess Diana. But almost as soon as it had begun, the home-coming celebration was spoiled by criticisms voiced by his father when the topic of his son's visit to Miami came up. Pedro angrily reiterated to Carlos the same old arguments about using his godsent talent to make his way in life, thinking of nothing or no one else, and he strongly reminded Carlos to forget his relatives, his home and all its problems, and concentrate one hundred per cent on his work. He astutely recognised that Carlos' serious injury had a lot to do with his mental state at meeting up with his long-lost relatives and the hurt they had inflicted on the Acosta family. He saw that the week-long visit to Miami had left his gifted young son saddened, confused and unable to focus properly. Despite pleas from the other family members who wanted to rejoice in Carlos' return and hear of his life in the Western world, there was a heated verbal battle between the two men. Carlos, who was still muddled and fatigued by the very recent injury and operation, vehemently repeated his desire to be a normal part of the Acosta family and not spend his life dancing, away from his much-loved mother and sister. But Pedro would hear none of it and the two said cruel things to each other before angrily separating. The outburst put a real dampener on the excitement of being home again. Saddened, Carlos, as he had always done since he was a little boy, went up to the rooftop to talk to his one remaining pigeon, before setting it free to fly away forever, away from its imprisonment – and wishing he could follow.

It would be almost a year before he danced again. Despite his father's attempts to have the local witch doctor offer up animal sacrifices and potions to heal the injury – all of which failed – Carlos returned to hospital to have a second operation. After slow recuperation, he gingerly returned to the ballet studio of the Ballet Nacional where he began the slow process of restoring his lost technique. When he saw himself in the wall mirrors, he was horrified at the sight of his muscle loss, which had occurred after such a long period of inactivity. Determined to get back into condition, he persevered with the gruelling exercises each dancer has to do each day, and soon regained his shape and strength. As always, his former teacher Chery's wise and motherly wisdom was sought regarding his future plans, and she suggested that Carlos should go and talk to Madame Alonso with the thought of re-joining the company in Havana. Carlos was fearful that the director might hold a grudge about his unauthorised absence to dance with English National Ballet, but nevertheless girded up his courage and went to see her, thinking that, 'After all, at sixteen, I had won top prizes in competitions including the Grand Prix at the prestigious international competitions and was the most successful dancer they had had.'

Alicia Alonso has her office on the ground floor of the company's home base at Calzada 510 between

D and E Streets. The room is dark and warm, often very warm, as she is not a fan of air conditioning, and the only window is shuttered. For any young dancer not knowing what kind of reception he or she will receive, it can be a daunting place.

For Carlos, the interview was difficult and uncomfortable though he gratefully acknowledged, 'Alicia Alonso respected me when I talked to her, more than some other people.' However, while the interview resulted in him being accepted into the company, it was only as a soloist, four ranks lower than the principal status he had held in London. It was obviously a means of making him feel humbled, and while he was grateful for her benevolence, it was no easy thing for him to accept loss of status. Deeply disappointed, he once more sought out Chery who told him to accept the situation meekly, to work hard, prove himself and let his technique show his ability. That advice was good and he obeyed. His foot hurt him less and less and, inspired by the other excellent male dancers in the company who exuded convincing machismo and raw athleticism, executed with relish and passion from their securely schooled base, he made every effort each day until he reached his own high standards once again.

It took over a whole year from the time that he had last danced at English National Ballet until he was given his first big role with Ballet Nacional de Cuba.

But at last Carlos was ready physically and mentally. He was just twenty when he danced *Le Corsaire* with as much gusto and flair as he could muster, given the interruption in his career, but he knew in his heart, even with the Cuban audience's enthusiastic reception, that his performance had certainly not been up to his best standards.

His next performance was in the entertaining narrative ballet of *Coppélia,* where he danced the role of Franz, the young boy who falls in love with a life-size doll. Here he partnered his old London flatmate Lourdes Novoa who had also returned to Cuba and was back with the company. The Acosta family was able to come and see him perform at last, and he felt proud that he could show them his best style. The success of this performance gave him hope that things were at last starting to look up and that his career was now on an upward swing, with him again being in the public eye. But he had more to learn about life in a ballet company and how it is made up of many individuals who all vie for the big parts. His next role was certainly not what he was dreaming of, and it taught him a huge lesson in the need of sometimes having to put personal ambition aside.

Instead of being given the expected lead in Jorge Lefebre's ballet *Oedipus Rex*, a role that was known for its great opportunities of interpretation, Carlos saw his name down on the cast list to perform the role of an eighty-year-old man who hobbles with a stick and gets hanged at the end of the ballet. The most galling thing for him was that his family had planned to come to see him dance and here he would be, not as a youth flying high and stunning the audience with his pyrotechnical feats, but shuffling around the stage in dirty rags. He grew very downhearted and once more sought out Chery for sympathy. She, however, reminded him that he had to have patience during these trying early days in the company when his progress seemed slower than he wanted. She also told him some home truths about being an artist, especially as someone like him who had already been in the spotlight. She said that throughout his career, because he had so much to offer, he would come into contact with other dancers and directors who would be jealous and envious of his abilities, and try to thwart him at every opportunity. But, she counselled, he had to learn to ride those waves, ignoring all temptation to fear them and to show his true spirit. He listened to her wise words and felt better again. And then, three weeks later, as if it was a positive proof of Chery's confidence in his future, Carlos received a letter from Ben Stevenson, the British choreographer he had met in London and who had verbally invited him to Texas. This time however it was a formally written invitation to join Houston Ballet, in the position of principal. And this time Carlos had no doubts and said yes immediately.

A week later Ben Stevenson flew in to Havana to set the wheels in motion. 'Carlos picked me up in his broken-down Volkswagen,' Stevenson related. 'It was a bumpy ride – and not only because of the potholes. Carlos then informed me he hadn't passed his driving test yet nor did he have insurance. My heart sank especially when we saw a policeman ahead on the rickety road who proceeded to stop us. But it was only to say hi to Carlos and ask how he was, and then we went off again. It was quite an experience!' Stevenson had come to see Carlos dance and to ask permission from Alicia Alonso for him to go to Texas. 'I have a lot of respect for Alicia and for what she has done for Cuba and for its dance in the years past. I talked to her and told her my plans for Carlos. And she said that he could come to us for three to six months. I don't know if the reason she agreed so readily was that she realised that it was impossible to get a visa in Havana since there was no American consulate in Cuba. But I knew that Carlos was going on tour with the company to Spain and that he could get one there. So I set the plan in motion and contacted my lawyer who said he could arrange for a work visa for the Cuban to be picked up by him in Madrid. Carlos came back with me to my hotel and over dinner I gave him the details of working at Houston Ballet.'

This included a long list of repertoire and information on the other dancers in the company and also the contract that Stevenson was offering. It was eye-popping to the young penniless Cuban. Health and dental insurance was included; there was a forty-four week company season and he'd have permission (with pay) to dance with other companies for two weeks a year. Then he discovered that he was being offered a salary that included far more zeros on the end of a figure than he, as a Cuban, could have ever imagined earning, especially since he was at present getting the equivalent of one dollar a month for dancing with Ballet Nacional de Cuba.

The company tour to Spain was long and tiring with many rehearsals and performances every day. Carlos made his debut in the principal roles of *Swan Lake, Giselle* and *Don Quixote* at the Albéniz Theatre in Madrid and was kept very busy. But it was exhausting for another reason and that was entirely of his own doing. Nightly he and the other dancers would frequent the salsa clubs where the popular Cuban boys would dazzle on the dance floor with their captivating moves and suave style. All the Spanish girls wanted to dance with them and they would stay until the early hours of the morning, return to the hotel and sleep for a few hours before starting the next full day of dancing with the rituals of class, rehearsals and performance at night. If they were tired here in the

Spanish capital, it was their own fault. But it was well worth it.

The day finally arrived for him to go to the American Embassy to apply for his work permit to dance with Houston Ballet. He had to get up early to wait in line outside the embassy after a highly successful performance the night before in the leading role as the roguish and audacious Basilio in *Don Quixote*. The audience had gone wild with his dancing and the applause had gone on for a long time. Now he was standing unrecognised on the street like an immigrant. He was certain that his request would be rejected and was very fearful that he would be turned away and embarrassed. He convinced himself that because Cuba and America had no relations with each other, obtaining a work visa would be impossible. Yet Stevenson had told him, 'Nothing is impossible with the right lawyer to sort things out.' Now clutching all the papers that Stevenson had sent and thoughtfully filled out for him, he waited his turn. Finally he was led in and at last made it up to the issuing agent's desk. His heart sank as a woman grimly looked at him as she took his forms. Seeing her face, he felt even more nervous that his was a hopeless request and that his application was going to be rejected. Worse still, that the news of his attempt to obtain an American visa would leak out and he would be in big trouble. 'She's not going to stamp the papers,' he panicked. Then, as so often happened in his life, it was his dancing that saved the day. As the woman studied the papers more thoroughly, her face changed as she looked up at him again. Her features became softer. She actually smiled. Apparently, she had attended the ballet performance of *Don Quixote* the night before and suddenly realised who it was that was in front of her. She turned and called the whole office to come over and meet the wonderful dancer about whom she had been telling them. Now there were big smiles all around, but none greater than on the face of Carlos the Cuban dancer, as he watched his application getting the official seal of approval and his passport stamped with the invaluable visa which allowed him to work in America. He was now ready for his next adventure.

8

Houston: We Have Lift-off

'The arrival of the Cuban Missile'

WHEN TWENTY-YEAR-OLD CARLOS arrived in Texas to start his new life in the autumn of 1993, he was amazed at what he saw. The city of Houston, made rich by its oil and famous for its space centre, seemed like a fantasy world to the poor boy from the back-streets of Cuba despite brief earlier experience of the outside world in South America, Europe and Miami. Texas was very different. Driving into Houston, the fourth largest city in the US, from the George Bush Intercontinental Airport, one's first impression is of a drab and flat nondescript landscape, long straight highways, tacky storefronts and scattered homes of uninteresting architecture. Then suddenly, like some fantastical stage set, the downtown area rises up like

Atlantis on the horizon. Strange-shaped skyscrapers are stacked together, the glass from their buildings glinting – and definitely hinting of money – in the bright sunshine. Wealth is omnipresent in this city and very visible, not only from these soaring buildings but also from the shining cars, the over-flowing stores, the well-dressed residents and especially the huge mansions that abound in the leafy streets near to the ballet studio. The inhabitants of many of those luxurious homes are all important to the city's ballet company – the Houston Ballet – especially since they are the valuable supporters and sponsors who keep the company alive financially and physically. Now the Houstonians were about to witness another lift-off in their city proud of its NASA Space Center, though this time it was of the superhuman kind, one who would blast skywards in action and reputation.

Despite its well-worn Hollywood film image as the land of cowboys and its geographical distance from the artistic activities of the east and west coasts of America, the state of Texas is no cultural backwater. In fact it is the opposite – it is alive with the arts, and no place more than Houston, which prides itself with its own first-class orchestra, opera and ballet companies.

Houston Ballet, today considered America's fourth top classical ballet company, gave its first performances in 1968 with just sixteen dancers, and five performances a year. Ben Stevenson took over the company eight years later and during his tenure – and in Carlos' time there – the company expanded to fifty-one dancers with more than eighty performances a year, and a budget of eleven million dollars. But outside of America, little was known about the company until the arrival of that 'Cuban missile'.

The artistic success of Houston Ballet from 1976 to 2003 can be attributed to Stevenson's wisdom, perspicacity and knowledge. His own high classical standards were quickly instilled in the company and during his twenty-seven years in the driving seat, he produced a great number of brilliant dancers, many of whom won medals at international competitions. He is renowned for his keen eye to spot new talent – the ultimate example was getting Carlos before the international world caught wind of the boy's stardom-in-the-making.

Due to Houston Ballet's excellent press department, the pre-arrival publicity buzzed with gleaned information of this young dancer's abilities. Before the city had seen him dance a single step, his name was blazoned in the headlines of the local papers. The public was fascinated by all the 'poor-boy-to-superstar' stories, and later, even hard-hearted journalists were won over by Carlos' honesty and simplicity when he gave interviews. Stevenson insisted that it was made very clear from the outset by immigration attorney Charles Foster that Carlos was not in any way defecting from his homeland, but that he was entering the United States legally on an 01 Temporary Work Visa.

Carlos arrived on Friday, 12 November 1993 and was thrust immediately into the heart of Texan-style generosity when Ben Stevenson invited him to stay at his home overlooking the sea in Galveston until he got settled. The headquarters of the company where Carlos worked was in the expensive River Oaks area, on the pleasant if busy West Gray Street. Here, the stark, grey and white building disguised the world of beauty and elegance that lay therein. As Carlos climbed the stairs that first morning, he wondered what standard of dancing he would find and, most of all, if he would fit in with the other dancers?

The company's exuberant Afro-American principal ballerina Lauren Anderson remembers his first appearance in the studios. 'I thought, "what a nice boy and what a nice smile", and then I saw him dance, and was amazed at his physicality and raw explosive exciting talent. And what machismo! Carlos is very charming and witty, and one respects him a great deal because, with all that natural talent and physical capability, he still works very hard. It's almost as if he believes he has none. He fitted in with us all immediately because he is very human.'

Once in the studio, and under the watchful eyes of Stevenson who was giving class that first morning (and the sideways glances of the other dancers), Carlos started to execute the daily *barre* exercises, going through the well planned rituals that slowly and precisely warm and strengthen each and every muscle.

It was in the Houston studios that Nina Ananiashvili, then the internationally famous Bolshoi Ballet prima ballerina and now artistic director of the State Ballet of Georgia, met Carlos for the first time when she was guesting with the company. Though she has danced with many of the ballet world's greatest male dancers during her own stunning career, she had some favourable comments to make about that initial sighting of Carlos. 'When I first saw him I was very impressed by the fact that, though he was already so technical, he still was staying after class in the studio working on his technique. What also impressed me was when he told me that Ben had taught him how to move and artistically present himself on stage, and how important that lesson was for him. This was very unusual and very pleasant to hear from such a young dancer. So many dancers think they do it all by themselves. But Carlos was naturally humble and receptive, and I admired that.'

When the dancers have completed the *barre* exercises, their bodies warmed, their muscles stretched, they go into the centre of the room for more exercises.

The routine here, as in all classical ballet classes, consists of elegant *port de bras* exercises for the upper body and short adagio sequences worked out by the teacher, which test the dancers' balance and ability to stand and turn on one leg. And there are small allegro steps in which the dancers have to use their feet nimbly and accurately. These the Houston dancers completed well, self-critically checking their posture and positioning of limbs in the huge wall mirrors. Then it came time for the *grand allegro* – the big fast moves, with jumps and turns that lift the dancer into the air. And here the company's men were amazed at Carlos' seemingly effortless strength and power to soar high and stay airborne, and his physical skills that made him spin so fast. They all congratulated him. Yet Stevenson remained taciturn. He could see the potential but at that moment, in terms of a classical dancer, the young man's talent was still raw and needed to be tamed and finely tuned. Nevertheless, he knew that Carlos was going to make his audiences sit up in their seats.

It was a mutual partnership. Carlos needed Ben as much as Ben needed Carlos. Given the quantity of good male dancers in the Ballet Nacional de Cuba with all its traditions and hierarchy, Carlos, had he remained in Cuba, would probably have taken a long time to be offered regular principal roles. But now, here at Houston Ballet, Ben was willing to take the risk and throw him straight in. He realised also that Carlos could have chosen another path – that of the wandering guest star. He could have played on his competition successes and accepted invitations to perform at galas the world over where he would have been seen by thousands of people and certainly become rich and famous. But the gypsy lifestyle, going from place to place, and the lack of regular coaching, would have limited his performing progress to just the stupendous technique and gasping leaps that audiences expected from him. His performances could have become repetitive given the limited array of popular 'party-pieces' in the ballet repertoire. He needed a home base far from the international scene in which to develop the other skills that constitute a truly brilliant performer. And he needed a replacement for Chery, an eagle-eyed coach who would discipline and refine the untapped material he had to offer. Stevenson was that person and in the five years that Carlos was with Houston Ballet, the director built up in him a strong secure foundation and gave him every opportunity to develop his special talents.

Three weeks after joining the company, Carlos made his debut in *The Nutcracker*, the same production that he had danced at English National Ballet. Stevenson, against the expectations of the audience and the dancers, had decided to cast him for opening night with the company's much loved prima ballerina Janie Parker as the Sugar Plum Fairy, and with the small and vivacious Martha Butler taking the role of the Snow Queen. Janie had been Stevenson's muse, and had started in the company when the Englishman took over as director. Martha had trained at the Houston Ballet Academy before entering the company. Both ballerinas were highly popular with the Houston audiences. The performance was a huge success though this casting for Carlos' debut was a surprise to many. 'Everyone expected Ben to put us two black dancers together,' said Lauren Andersen laughing. 'But that was to come later.' The bubbly ballerina is a Houstonian, and product of the Houston Ballet Academy. Naturally, her many colleagues and audiences assumed that Lauren would automatically be paired with Carlos, but Stevenson liked to offer the unexpected. Where race was concerned, the director was colour blind. He looked at the individual dancer for qualities rather than skin tones. There was often initial surprise at some of his bold decisions from certain members of the audience, but his point was proved on stage. Unlike many other ballet directors who seek cardboard copies of dancers in height, looks and abilities for their companies, Stevenson built up the reputation of Houston Ballet on the uniqueness of each individual dancer.

During those first few months, there was a lot to learn and to work on and Carlos could be seen in many new roles. In March 1994, the company presented a triple bill in which he danced the fourth act of *La Bayadère* with Martha Butler. Together they made a delightful team, his secure partnering and her technical finesse embellishing the pristine splendour of this great work. In his solo, Carlos soared high and streaked around the stage in speedy stretched *jetés* which, combined with his elegant whizzing spins, made the audience go wild with enthusiasm.

As his reputation grew, so did demands for Carlos to appear in other countries, especially in gala concerts. Stevenson was willing to let him go for these short trips to fly the flag for Houston Ballet. And whenever he had any free time he would return to his native Cuba to see his family and to honour his contract to still dance with the company, where he would share information with his old colleagues about the dance world and repertoire in America.

The end of season saw Carlos dancing in two of the five diverse pieces on offer in Houston Ballet's 'Summer Sampler' – in the demanding one-act ballet *Études* by the Danish choreographer Harald Lander and later the *pas de deux* from *Don Quixote* with Lauren Anderson. The result here was like tinder to dry brushwood – their dancing ignited the stage. 'Carlos packed it with everything,' Lauren remembered afterwards. 'We had no idea then what that performance started,' while a newspaper noted that Carlos sliced the air with 'scissor-like leaps' and 'mercury-fast spins'.* Lauren matched him with her whipping turns. Their fiery and fun antics on the Wortham stage gave the delighted audience a taste for more – and the news was good. Stevenson stated that he was going to recreate the full three-act ballet of *Don Quixote* and that it would showcase this distinctive and thrilling partnership.

In his first year, the young Cuban had taken the Texan city and its citizens by storm. His virtuosity astounded and his natural charisma brought him Hollywood-style recognition. When out on the street, taxi drivers would honk and wave to him. In restaurants, fellow diners would come up to pat him on the back with a 'Howdy! Great show last night.' Even waitresses shyly asked for his autograph and were always rewarded with courtesy and a dazzling, sunshine-filled smile. Carlos never evidenced any sense of self-importance or pride and has remained a natural, generous, kind and polite individual throughout his career.

As soon as the season and his year's contract and visa ended, he set off for home and a family reunion. He was not planning to return to Texas despite being

---

* *Houston Chronicle*, 4 June 1994

offered another contract for the following season – his heart was still in Cuba and he had been home-sick away from his family. However, he now found Cuba riddled with problems – long daily power cuts, lack of food, and the standard of living barely above the poverty level. On top of this, people were leav-ing like lemmings by any means available – many by building their own rickety rafts or jumping into rub-ber tyres. And this time, the authorities were mak-ing little attempt to stop them. Yet, after a year away from friends and family, Carlos still hankered after his old life and was determined to stay. His amazed breakdancing friends told him he was mad to con-template staying on the poverty-stricken island when he had work, money and a good life outside. Chery had organised for him to have an apartment of his own and he took pride in buying the basic equip-ment. Soon his sister Berthe and then his mother joined him and he was happy to have company. Alas, Berthe's schizophrenia took hold once more and she attempted to throw herself into the sea from the Malecón – the long sea wall that rambles around Havana. Instead, she landed on the sharp rocks suf-fering severe injuries to her legs, and was taken to hospital where she had pins put into her limbs. Car-los, true to past form, felt that he should have been more aware of her distress and resolved that his place was in Cuba. However, Pedro talked with him, this time in a serious and calm manner, and after much soul-searching the young dancer decided to take his father's advice and concentrate only on his ballet life, so he rejoined Ballet Nacional. Then he found that he was included on its annual tour to Spain, which meant he would have another opportunity to apply for an American visa. It was a tough decision to make but he plucked up courage to tell Madame Alonso that Stevenson had invited him back and she finally agreed to his request. He immediately contacted the director asking him to prepare the visa papers as he had done the year before. Carlos was returning to America. It was great news for Houston Ballet and for its audiences.

And it was no surprise when Stevenson crafted his new *Don Quixote* on the talents of his two extrovert black dancers – though there were also four other pairs of principals who brought different, exciting qualities to the two roles. Based freely on Miguel de Cervantes' novel, the scenario makes a showy ballet, full of action, adventures and much humour. Stevenson's extravagant production was an immediate success. It premiered on 15 February 1995 (aptly during America's annual Black History Month) with the two black superstars in the leading roles – and they produced an electrifying performance. The more experienced Lauren was not to be outdone by twenty-one-year-old Carlos whose relentless display of flawless technical feats 'matched Anderson step for step while bringing Basilio to full and vibrant life.'* Lauren recalled: 'We busted out every move there is in *Don Q*. We had fun doing it. When he did quadruple turns in second position [turning on one leg with the other held straight out to the side at ninety degrees] I did triple *fouettés* [a whipping turn on one leg on *pointe* that requires stability and control]. And so on. From then, the competition was on!' The audience loved their highly charged competitiveness and urged them on with their applause. They became the darlings of the ballet.

In the 1995–96 season, the company went off on tour to China where Carlos danced his first Romeo. However the *Houston Press* criticised him for his poor acting skills. The Texas dance critic Margaret Puttnam noted that 'his physical control, the strength of his movements and his sheer princely presence are surprising for a performer so young. But his acting has a ways to go.'† Carlos' youthful eagerness to dazzle with his technique alone made him lose sight of the unfolding drama with all its implications. Once recognised, he worked on the characterisation until he became naturally convincing. Romeo has since become one of his most endearing and most notable

---

* *Houston Press*, Mitchell J. Shields, 2 March 2005
† *Houston Press*, 14 March 1996

roles. At the end of that season, he partnered Janie in *The Sleeping Beauty* for her farewell performance. It was a stunning if poignant evening – Janie still showing exquisite style and elegance, while Carlos, making his debut as Florimund, was memorable for his gracious princely manners and breathtaking, sky-high cabrioles and swift pirouettes.

Carlos continued to partner Lauren much to the delight of the Houstonian crowds and beyond. The exuberant couple scored more triumphs in 1995 when they were invited to dance in a gala in Russia. Olga Guardia Smoak, a Panamanian-born American and international representative of the Jackson Mississippi Ballet Competition, was living in Moscow at that time, working as the English editor of the Russian ballet magazine *Balyet*. Having seen them dance in Jackson, she suggested their names to the gala committee. 'There was a moment's hesitation as there had never been black dancers in Russian galas,' she related. 'But I was insistent that everyone would love them.' The couple duly received an invitation to perform – and Ben's permission to go. Recognising the importance of their appearance in a country where classical ballet was truly treasured – and dissected – Lauren reported: 'By the time we got to Russia, we had caged our energy and refined our artistry and technique.' It was a long flight from Houston to Moscow both mentally and physically, and they were exhausted when they finally arrived in the Russian capital. Yet, according to Olga Smoak, despite his weariness, 'Carlos was a ray of sunshine – always in a tremendous mood.' The gala, 'Diamonds in the World of Dance', was held in the mammoth seven-thousand-seat Palace of Congresses, situated in the walled 'city' of the Kremlin. The Houston duo chose to dance the popular and dynamic *Diana and Actaeon pas de deux*, which allowed them to display their incredible facilities of earth-devouring leaps and jumps as they swept across the truly enormous stage. Their performance won the hearts of the Muscovites who marvelled at the couple's easy and natural technical feats, and the *joie de vivre* of their dancing. After the show, there was a reception in a fashionable cafe, where Carlos was the life and soul of the party with his effervescent wit and humour, and of course, his fantastic salsa displays. Everyone wanted to dance with him.

This visit broke through any colour prejudice many of Russia's ballet-goers held, and a few months later, the couple was on the top of the list for another prestigious gala in the Russian capital. This time it was the ninetieth birthday celebration of Olga Lepeshinskaya, one of the Soviet Union's most popular ballerinas, and her gala evening was held at the historic Bolshoi Theatre. This magnificent building stands in Sverdlovsk Square, close to the Kremlin and Red

Square. Backstage, Carlos felt very much at home as the area was quite run-down, with peeling paint and splintery wooden floors – the whole theatre was about to undergo a massive restoration programme. Lauren vividly remembers the trip. 'The gala featured Madame Lepeshinskaya's own, now famous students, their students and the two of us. On the long flight over, Carlos and I talked about everything from slavery to Castro, and how, if it weren't for the Cuban government, the dancer we know as Carlos Acosta would not be here today. Anyway, we were to dance *Le Corsaire* and after class we got ready to do a practice run-through. It was not our best rehearsal. We had to make major adjustments as the uneven wooden stage floor was also raked quite steeply. Because we were not used to it, Carlos' quadruple turns in second position became doubles and my triple *fouettés* became singles and doubles. We took all the extra time we could in the studios to get used to the rake (in Russia, ballet stages slope slightly upwards from the front, whereas in most Western theatres, they are level). But we danced our best and had fun and it was obvious that Madame Olga and the audience enjoyed it. At the end of the concert, she came on stage, was inundated with bouquets of flowers and spoke to the audience. We had no idea what she was saying. She looked over at us and said something about us in Russian, but the only thing we sort of recognised was our names. Then a rather handsome gentleman in a suit came over and started translating for us, telling us that we were getting a glowing report from Madame Lepeshinskaya. Later we found out that this man was Vladimir Vasiliev (one of the Bolshoi's greatest male dancers, and at this time, director of the Bolshoi Theatre). The audience started screaming and applauding whenever our names were mentioned and it was fun to watch them. But most important for me was the comment that Carlos made quietly to me at that moment on stage. He said, "Lauren, look. They are applauding for two black ballet dancers." He smiled a big smile. I smiled with tears of joy and acceptance.'

Carlos got on well with his Houston colleagues – they called him Air Acosta (after the basketball player Michael Jordan whose nickname was Air Jordan because he could jump so high), and he taught many of them the secrets of good salsa dancing – and the best places in Houston to practise them. David Makhateli from the Republic of Georgia was also a member of Houston Ballet at this time. David, today a principal with The Royal Ballet in London, remembers his first meeting with Carlos. 'In 1997, I was a member of Dutch National Ballet when Carlos came as a guest to dance *The Nutcracker*. My friend Nina Ananiashvili had suggested I should go to Houston Ballet to further my career and repertoire, and I asked Carlos his opinion. He said that it would be a good experience, and when he returned to Houston, he put in a good word for me with Ben, and I got a contract. Carlos has been very helpful in many ways in my life. He has regularly helped me career- and technique-wise. He would inspire the other boys in Houston Ballet who would stay around after the class had ended to try all the tricks that he performed. The company looked up to him. They respected his achievements and the way he worked – and he always worked very hard. He is generous, funny and has a great sense of humour – the audiences just love him.'

Carlos was delighted when he was able to procure a visa for his mother to come and visit him. Sadly her stay was not as successful as he'd hoped. He had lost the scrap of paper on which he had written his relatives' phone number in Miami, which meant that a very disappointed María could not make the call to her mother that she had long dreamed about. Deeply saddened, she returned to Cuba earlier than planned and her shortened visit meant that she did not get to see her boy dance on the American stage, nor witness the reception he regularly received from his Texas fans. However, after she left, Carlos' foot started causing him problems again and he actually had to cancel his performances to have more treatment.

As his fame grew, so did the requests for him to make guest appearances in many cities and countries.

He was regularly being compared to the great Russian dancers Mikhail Baryshnikov and Rudolf Nureyev for the excitement he brought to stages worldwide. He was invited to dance in South America, the Far East, in Europe and all over the United States. He joined Nina Ananiashvili's group of international stars in Taiwan in 1996 and in Dallas a year later. In each of the venues where he danced, he produced the technical force and excitement that the public had paid to see.

In 1995, Carlos received a highly prestigious dance fellowship award from the Princess Grace Foundation, presented to him by Prince Rainier of Monaco, and in January 1997 he was invited back to Switzerland – one of six dancers – to perform in the twenty-fifth anniversary of the Prix de Lausanne where he elegantly partnered the Russian ballerina Diana Vishneva, another prizewinner who has become the leading ballerina of the Mariinsky Theatre.

In February 1997, back in Houston, Carlos' whole body was tested in a very un-classical way. He was selected to be the Chosen One in Glen Tetley's production of *The Rite of Spring*. The original ballet, *Le Sacre du Printemps,* created by Vaslav Nijinsky and premiered in Paris by the Ballets Russes in 1913, caused a riot when the French audience, unused to such tribal choreography, tried to drown the pounding rhythms of Igor Stravinsky's score with catcalls and boos. In Tetley's version of the pagan rituals, it is a youth rather than a maiden who is sacrificed to appease the gods in the frenzied dance that accelerates to the violent killing finale. For Carlos as the Chosen One, it was a powerful and exhausting role that demanded non-stop action: high leaping, explosive animalistic dancing and twirling with wild abandon. In the reincarnation scene, he literally took to the air in a flying harness. Wearing only tiny Speedos and body paint, his muscular, toned body didn't go unnoticed in the auditorium. He looked like a Greek god, glinting from his exertions in this very difficult and different role. Another of these contemporary works was Christopher Bruce's *Rooster*, a witty and engaging piece set to the music of The Rolling Stones. Now Carlos had to change his classical technique for jazzy, jerky and disjointed movements, hands on hips and elbows tucked out like wings, while pecking his head like a cockerel strutting in a farmyard. He wore tight skinny jeans, an overlarge suit jacket and thin tie just like the band's lead singer, Mick Jagger. He certainly looked king of the roost showing off to the 'chicks', and outdoing the other males with his hair-smarming and swagger.

Carlos was involved in creating two world premiere roles in Stevenson's ballets. The first of these was *Dracula* in 1997, where he danced Frederick, the other was

The Snow Maiden, his last big spectacular ballet with the company, created in March 1998, in which he was the peasant Misgir. In this full-length ballet adapted from the traditional Russian fairy tale, he danced with confidence and dare-devilry, offering pyrotechnical wizardry with many a Russian folk-dance trick included. Misgir's fiancée, the demure and sweet village girl Coupava was danced by Tiekka Schofield – Carlos' off-stage girlfriend – and she delivered some beautiful *fouettés* and pirouettes. Nina Ananiashvili performed a truly memorable Snow Maiden. She acted to perfection the beautiful but mischievous young girl from the icy kingdom, dancing with delicacy and true artistry. Nina stated that she loved the experience of working on the ballet. 'It was an exciting time with Houston Ballet. Ben Stevenson made his *Snow Maiden* ballet for Carlos and me. It was a very important experience because it was the first time that a ballet was especially staged for me and I was there right from the beginning. During the period when I was in Houston and we were working in the studio rehearsing, Carlos and I became good friends. He is a very good and strong partner and he's an easygoing, friendly person. I was very happy to invite him to perform in my galas and to come on tours in different countries.'

At the premiere's post-performance reception, conversation stopped when Carlos entered the room looking very handsome and elegant in fashionable clothes (his wide smile showing that the distinctive gap in his front teeth had been taken care of by a Houston dentist) with blonde Tiekka Schofield on his arm. All eyes focused on them as the two swept around the room greeting people. They made a remarkable and contrasting couple. Tiekka, a principal of Houston Ballet, was known for her quick mind and intelligence, and also her interest in so many issues from political to artistic affairs. On top of that she was tall, very beautiful and chic. And now there she was on the arm of the young man who had run barefoot throughout his neighbourhood, stolen mangoes and played truant from school. He also confessed to not having read a book until he was in his twenties. But it was obvious that the two were very much in love.

The ballet was a great success and the glowing reviews made a fitting tribute to the ending of Carlos' days in Texas. In his final press release the twenty-four-year-old stated, 'I love Houston Ballet and want to continue to dance in Texas. This company is like family to me and Houston audiences have been very kind to me. At the same time, I'm really young and I'd like to work with other people. A gift is a responsibility. You have to share it with everybody.'

Now he was to do just that, jetting off across the Atlantic to join the prestigious Royal Ballet with Tiekka at his side.

9

Slow Beginnings Lead to Speedy Progress

'It has been heaven to have him in the company'

AS HAD HAPPENED BEFORE, it was connections – to say nothing of qualifications – that got Carlos the job at The Royal Ballet in London's Royal Opera House. 'I had danced – and danced very well – at the Prix de Lausanne's twenty-fifth anniversary closing gala in Switzerland. It was there that I met Jay Jolley (the assistant director of The Royal Ballet School) and I asked him about the possibility of joining the company,' Carlos explained. Having danced with Houston Ballet for five years and feeling that he had danced practically every work, he was ready for a change. Now he cast his eyes across the Atlantic.

The Royal Ballet boasts a treasure house bursting

with choreographic gems, works both old and new, and for a serious dancer like Carlos, and indeed for many of the world's top dancers, the enticement of joining the company was great. Carlos duly received an invitation to come to London and take an audition doing morning class with the company's dancers, and in May 1998 he flew over from Houston.

At that time The Royal Ballet Company studios were to be found at Barons Court, in a less than salubrious location by the Hammersmith flyover where non-stop traffic roars out of London to the southwest. The redbrick building that the company shared with the Upper School students was the place where Carlos was first seen, but if he caused interest, he didn't know it. The company got on with their daily routines and barely looked at him. No official seemed to be watching, so, he wondered, why was he here? Finally towards the end of the exercises, Anthony Dowell, then the artistic director of the company entered the studio. He had been The Royal Ballet's definitive *danseur noble* for more than twenty years, a dancer of great finesse and beautiful technique. His assistant Monica Mason, who had been one of the company's much-loved ballerinas, followed him in. (She would take over the full reins of directorship in 2002.) They watched silently, without a hint of expression on their faces. 'I'd heard of Carlos from Ben Stevenson whom I'd known in the fifties,' said Monica Mason.

'He talked a lot about him, so I was eager to see the boy. I wasn't disappointed. He's the most wonderful "rain-shower" of joy which he spreads around him.'

After class, Carlos was invited to a discussion in the director's office where he was offered a contract for the season beginning in September 1998. 'Both of us were very happy to have him join us. We could see that he would be a great addition to the company,' continued Ms Mason. Carlos was to become The Royal Ballet's first black principal dancer.

Carlos was overjoyed at the prospect of joining, but he had one great anxiety – Tiekka. Happily, she told him she was willing to come to London with him and look for a job there. The next duty was also very hard – to tell Ben Stevenson. Though the British director must have realised the inevitable probability of Carlos leaving Houston at some point, it was a severe blow. Carlos had raised the profile of his company to new heights and the names of Acosta and Houston Ballet had become synonymous for quality and excitement. It was not the easiest of meetings but it was done. And Carlos still had more ballets to perform and audiences to please before the Houston season ended.

At the end of June and fresh from numerous triumphs throughout Texas, Carlos paid a quick visit back to Cuba to see his family and introduced them to Tiekka. Then the couple, accompanied by fourteen pieces of luggage, flew off for London where Carlos would take up his new, and hopefully, exciting contract with The Royal Ballet. Despite their high hopes of a spanking new future, there was not to be an auspicious beginning for either of them.

Coming from a city where he was known and loved by outsiders as well as the ballet public, Carlos now found himself thrust in the midst of people who seemed uninterested in the 'new boy'. Monica Mason suggested later: 'It was probably because people feel reticent about being chummy with a principal, and also, at that time, there were few Spanish speakers.' The naturally ebullient Cuban found it hard having to prove himself once more, especially given all the successes and adulation he had had in his past life. Unlike Houston, there seemed to be a moratorium on news features about ballet dancers and he grew anxious that nothing was reported about his arrival in Britain – The Royal Ballet at that time wasn't over keen on the 'celebrity' story angle.

His spirits lifted when he got a message from Cuba asking him to come to Paris to dance *Swan Lake* with his old company Ballet Nacional, and with Lorna Feijoo as his Odette/Odile. As the Royal's season had not started he was able to accept, taking Tiekka with him, and was delighted with the reception he received in the French capital – the first time he had been back since he won the Grand Prix in 1990. 'It was great to dance there and be with my friends again. And Alicia also thanked me very much for coming to dance,' he said gratefully. It was always important to keep in her good graces. Flushed with success he returned to London to find that he was making his Royal debut in an ultra-modern work by William Forsythe, an American choreographer and director of Ballet Frankfurt. *In the Middle, Somewhat Elevated* is a gritty, fast-paced look at the classical ballet technique with a modernist eye. The steps are speedy, off-centre, arms and legs flailing in every direction with stabbing kicks, hips askew and arms stretched out with wrists flexed upwards. All this was performed to a deafening electronic score punctuated with metallic music. Carlos was certainly up to these new challenges, danced well and was noticed. But it was not what he had expected to be first seen in. He had presumed in his debut with The Royal Ballet that he would be showing the British public his classical wizardry. He had to learn to be patient, to learn that it takes time for the British fervour to ignite, and it can be an infuriatingly long wait before it gets going. But when it does, it explodes with fiery enthusiasm, making the wait all the more worthwhile. This was to happen, but in his first few months, it seemed a far-off aspiration.

Carlos soon discovered that he had arrived in

London at one of the bleakest periods in the Royal Opera House's history. As if joining a new company in a new city and setting up home was not enough, he found that morale with his new fellow dancers was at an all-time low. The Royal Opera House closed for expensive and extensive renovation in 1997 and, as the theatre management had not found an alternative home for the dancers during the expected two years of rebuilding, there was much restlessness. The Royal Ballet, without a home base, made for a challenging time for the whole company. Like wandering gypsies, the dancers found they were performing in various locations more suited to lavish 'one-night-only' productions, or else they were touring the country in small groups. And they found that many of the stages they had to perform on were not really equipped for ballet. In London they appeared in such places as the Hammersmith Apollo – a huge barn of a building better equipped to deal with pop shows than *pointe* shoes – and the Royal Festival Hall, a concert hall with a wide stage that offers little depth and has no wings. Carlos' debut in Forsythe's piece was at the pre-renovated Sadler's Wells Theatre in Islington.

'In Houston,' explained Carlos, 'I was dancing an average of twenty shows in two months. But now I discovered that I only had ten shows in five months and no First Nights. It was terrible and so bad for morale as well as for my technique.' There were niggling thoughts that perhaps he had made a huge mistake in leaving America. He reflected on his new life on this side of the Atlantic and on his difficulty in making friends, which was basically a misunderstanding of that British character trait which, unlike the over-effusive spirit of the Cuban people, takes its time to warm up to newcomers. Added to his worries was the news that Tiekka had not been accepted at either The Royal Ballet or English National Ballet and eventually accepted a contract with Scottish Ballet, a respected company based in Glasgow, but a long way from London. Now there was no one at home after a hard day with whom to share his troubles. His lack of fluency in the language meant that he missed out on the camaraderie of others, so he threw himself into his work to compensate and to express himself. After all, he had come to London to learn new roles and he was determined that nothing should deter him from achieving his goal. Then he had news that sent his spirits to a new low. Tiekka had suddenly returned to Texas after suffering an injury while rehearsing. Unable to reach him as he was in the studio in Covent Garden, she had caught the first plane back to Houston to have her foot operated on. The weeks passed and it eventually became obvious that their relationship had broken down for good. It was a terrible blow for him. 'It seemed unimaginable now looking back,' he bemoaned. 'But here I was, starting in a new

Apollo

With Darcey Bussell in *Apollo*

La Fille Mal Gardée

Romeo and Juliet

With Tamara Rojo in *Romeo and Juliet*

With Tamara Rojo in *Diana and Actaeon*

Diana and Actaeon

Diana and Actaeon

With
Viengsay
Valdés in *Le
Corsaire*

With Viengsay Valdés in *Swan Lake*

With Viengsay Valdés in *Swan Lake*

La Bayardère

Requiem – Offertoire

Spartacus

Spartacus

Tocororo

Tocororo

In class in Cuba, 2006

Carlos with his nephew Yonah in Cuba, 2006

Premières

Premières

company, working in a new environment and experiencing a new culture and with no special friends. That was tough. And now, I had no girlfriend. If all this was not bad enough, there was the British weather. Oh, how I missed the sunshine. We Cubans cannot live without it.' But fortunately, he pulled himself together and stayed, immersing himself even deeper into his work, imbuing it with his own pent-up feelings and passion. With the lure of the Royal's fantastic array of classical and contemporary works set out like a sumptuous banquet before him, his sense of professionalism and desire to expand his knowledge kept him going. He hid his dark feelings and doggedly determined to learn what he could. His father's advice, unwelcome in his youth, was now uppermost in his mind as he remembered that he must not spend time and energy looking back. He must take every opportunity offered him and think how he could make it his own. He worked harder than he had ever done, keeping to himself and concentrating only on improving his style and technique.

After his contemporary beginning, his next appearance was purely classical. Here in the third act divertissement of *Raymonda,* staged by Rudolf Nureyev, he was, at last, able to show his finesse and detailed technique, as well as exciting bravura with spectacular one-handed lifts.

A big test came in January 1999 when he was given

the role of Colas in Frederick Ashton's *La Fille Mal Gardée* and the choreography was different from anything that he had danced before. This well-loved family ballet is set in the rolling English countryside with delightful 'chickens' that scratch and peck, a real live pony and trap and a joyous scenario that keeps the audience chuckling. Carlos danced the penniless hero in love with Lise, a wayward young girl who disrupts her widowed mother's plans for her to marry the squire's eccentric son, Alain. Carlos' interpretation of Colas, which he has now danced many times, has been called 'irresistibly charming and with the confidence to sweep any girl off her feet'.* Ashton, who laid the foundations of the English style, fills his works with musicality, lyricism and deceptively difficult technique. The footwork is rapid and precise while the head, arms and upper body embellish the appearance. The steps in the male solos are intricate, and the bravura technique has to be done with lightness and bounce in the *ballon* (small jumps), all at a fast pace – a style that has regularly defeated even the most talented dancer. But not Carlos, who seized the challenge with relish. The bucolic atmosphere in which you almost smell the pure, fresh country air makes *Fille* a happy ballet to watch and one that Carlos has continued to enjoy over the years. '*Fille* like

---

* Jane Simpson in *Dance Now* Spring 2005

Cinderella is one of a very few feel-good ballets,' he said. 'It's a bit silly but you just feel happy throughout and smile, so it makes a nice change from all those dramatic and dark works that we do. But yes, I am never at ease in those yellow tights that Colas has to wear – not with my thighs.' He laughed loudly.

At the end of 1999, after nearly two years of being on the road, the Royal Opera House was re-opened and The Royal Ballet was able to return to its old familiar stage – now all spruced up and re-modelled – and to the wonderful new facilities at the top of the building where airy large studios and fresh bright dressing rooms awaited them. No more dashing from class at Barons Court to catch the Piccadilly line to Covent Garden for company rehearsals. To celebrate its £214 million refurbishment and reopening, the Royal Opera House staged a three-hour glittering gala on 1 December attended by HM Queen Elizabeth II, HM the Queen Mother, and other dignitaries. Sharing the evening with the Royal Opera, The Royal Ballet celebrated its history with old films and with twenty-three mini extracts of well-loved works depicting special ballet moments and personalities who had brought fame to the company. Carlos was delighted to discover that he was to represent arguably the greatest male dancer of our time, the Tatar-born, Russian-trained Rudolf Nureyev who had joined The Royal Ballet eight months after his defection from the Kirov Ballet tour in Paris in 1991. His superlative dancing had raised the image of the male dancer, transforming it from being the support and partner of the ballerina into an equal and veritable force in the terpsichorean art. Although Carlos had never seen him dance other than on film, he recognised the honour he had been given and determined to show his best. Dancing the solo from *Le Corsaire* he was equally impressive, soaring through the air, covering the stage with long powerful leaps, slicing the air with razor-sharp *jetés* before ending with fast spinning turns. The audience loved it and he received thunderous applause. The gala was also shown on BBC television, so many more thousands spotted him for the first time and liked what they saw. He had made his mark at last.

Back in the Opera House, Carlos was pleased to be getting more new and challenging roles that showed the public that he was also an excellent, expressive actor. His first Kenneth MacMillan ballet was *My Brother, My Sisters* – a dark scenario about incestuous feelings between siblings and a resulting death. His absorption and unspoken acceptance of the unfolding situation made the ballet compulsive watching. Carlos was to demonstrate again and again in MacMillan's many works, how his magnetic presence and superb dancing brought the ballets to life. 'I really wish that I had been able to work with him,' he said sadly. 'I think we would have done well together.' (Indeed, MacMillan who died in 1992, would most likely have been delighted to create works for someone of Carlos' calibre.) 'MacMillan's works are so theatrical,' Carlos continued. 'He sometimes uses just a gesture or even a completely still moment to convey the mood needed, whereas Ashton's choreography is always moving and is more classical.'

The 1999–2000 season gave Carlos many opportunities to expand his skills and he was happy in the new roles that he was given to learn. This, after all, was the reason he had come to London. The Opera House also benefited – his name on the cast list became a sign that there would be a full house. In July 2000, he made his debut as Des Grieux, the lovelorn poet in MacMillan's tragic and romantic ballet *Manon* and also in *Song of the Earth*, a profoundly serious and moving ballet in which Carlos depicted the Messenger of Death. In these deeply dramatic roles, Carlos recognised that he had a range of real-life experiences that separated him from most other ballet exponents. He could bring to his performances strong, sincerely felt emotions, many of which he had personally experienced. All those years of loneliness, desperation, of feeling unloved were now pulled up from the depths to be used to enhance his performances. That meant, when he danced a role, he was not presenting the same Carlos dressed in a different costume, as some dancers tend to do. Now he poured himself into each different character seeking out the very soul of the role he was to dance. He was also very aware that his physical abilities to jump high and hover in the air, and his speedy spinning on the spot were very distinctive. This dynamic style had been one of the trademarks that set him apart at school and had won him top prizes. And while audiences came to delight in his exhilarating power-horse action, the new skills he was developing showed them the serious and sincere artist he was truly becoming.

There was bitter disappointment when Carlos discovered that when MacMillan's *Romeo and Juliet* returned to the repertoire, he had been given the role of Mercutio. Was it because the British public still found it hard to accept a black Romeo or prince, he pondered? Many years later he was questioned about this on a Cuban television show and he spoke candidly and in great detail about the need for directors to see the ability of a dancer rather than skin colour. 'When it comes to choosing a prince for a ballet, we must emphasise that it is not a question of being black, no, it is a question of whether a black or mulatto dancer has the talent to bring to the prince or hero role. So give them the chance to surprise.'*

---

* *Con 2 que se quieran*, compered by Amauri Perez, 20 April 2010

It would be another eight years – March 2006 – before he was to become the first black dancer in The Royal Ballet's history to dance Romeo. Fortunately a production with Carlos and the brilliant Spanish ballerina Tamara Rojo as the two young Shakespearian lovers has been filmed for posterity, and Romeo has become one of Carlos' most endearing roles. He brings youthful infatuation and deep romantic passion to his character, along with superb and sublime dancing. The duo continues to make a dream partnership on stage, which started when Tamara first joined The Royal Ballet for the 2000–01 season.

'The first big ballet we did together was *Swan Lake*,' she recalls. 'We knew each other from before as, when I was young, I had seen Carlos dance in Madrid and he was the new star of the Ballet Nacional de Cuba. He took some classes in my school and I remember thinking he had something special, difficult to pin down, different from everybody else. Of course, we also share culture and language so we understand each other very quickly.' The two have danced together all over the world and are very popular. Their performances are exciting, of the highest quality and the finest dancing. Tamara is another of those ballerinas who can stun by the quantity and speed of her pirouettes, her pure classical technique and her powerful dramatic ability to draw the audience into her characters. And they sometimes get the same buzz of excitement off-stage. Tamara laughs, recalling one time they set off to perform abroad.

'Some years ago, we were invited to do a gala in Mexico City. We were to do two *pas de deux* – from *Le Corsaire* and from *Manon* – and it was winter. The flight was London-Paris-Mexico. Because we both had shows at the Opera House, we could only fly the day before so we went very early to the airport to find that Paris was closed due to a snowstorm. We waited for some hours and finally were told that our flight had been rescheduled for the following day, which meant we would arrive in Mexico just in time for the show, with no time to prepare. So I did my make-up and hair on the plane. Can you imagine what other passengers thought about that?' she giggled. 'Naturally, the plane was late, and by the time we arrived in Mexico City, the show had already started. The organisers had now decided that we would open and close the second part of the gala. A car was waiting for us by the steps of the plane, the driver drove in a totally crazy way to the theatre. During the drive, Carlos had his feet in a bucket of ice and water to reduce the swelling from the flight. We arrived at the theatre, quickly talked to the conductor (we had not had time to rehearse with the orchestra and as they did not know which variation I was going to perform in *Corsaire*, they had worked out three different versions). Then we went on to the stage and danced in a total trance. After many, many performances and unusual situations I still think that was one of the best performances we have achieved. Even Mexico's altitude did not affect us!'

Just when life seemed to be more interesting, the directorship of The Royal Ballet changed. In 2001 Anthony Dowell stepped down and in his place the Royal Opera House Board appointed an Australian who had been assistant director at American Ballet Theatre in 1993 and director of Australian Ballet in 1997. His name was Ross Stretton and it was possibly the most unpopular appointment that the Royal Opera House Board of Directors has made.

Stretton's plans for the company set many Royal bona fide supporters' teeth on edge. For a start, he gave many of the coveted and long-awaited major roles to the younger members of the company while the more qualified dancers like Carlos were dubbed 'dead wood' and barely used at all. 'Ross didn't like me and he didn't want a confrontation with any of us experienced dancers,' commented Carlos. 'I was getting so little to do – so I decided that I would try to work somewhere else and set off for Manhattan to audition for American Ballet Theatre. I was so anxious about my future that I was ready to make a commitment with ABT.' Fortunately for The Royal Ballet there was a coup in the company and Ross Stretton was dismissed before his contract was up. Monica Mason, who had always been a great supporter of Carlos and was ready to encourage his development and exposure on stage, replaced Stretton and became the artistic director of The Royal Ballet. 'I was in New York when Monica called, telling me, "This is your home. Come back." So I returned.' In 2002, Carlos and Tamara Rojo opened the new season dancing *La Bayadère*. It was a spectacular performance from both of them.

This appointment as director proved to be an excellent one. Monica Mason, a South African by birth, has fifty-two years of experience with the company, as a dancer, teacher, coach, assistant director and now artistic director. Being so strongly steeped in the traditions of The Royal Ballet and its history, she has been aware of nurturing its past repertoire while opening up the future to the dancers of today. 'Carlos was one of my priorities,' she told me. 'I knew he must be challenged and must feel fulfilled after having made such a huge leap to join our company. And I never doubted that he would be able to take on a variety of roles. He is intelligent, humble and has the desire to try anything we throw at him. In fact it has been heaven to have him in the company.'

Carlos' daily routine is always the same – arriving at the Royal Opera House, he goes first into the studio for the morning class taught by home-grown and guest teachers. One of the latter is Mikhail Messerer, ex-Bolshoi dancer whose family constitutes one of the great lineages in Russian classical ballet. He teaches worldwide and is now the ballet master in chief at the Mikhailovsky Ballet in St Petersburg. Asked about his connection with Carlos, he replied:

'I first met Carlos in Buenos Aires, where I was giving master classes and he came to do a guest performance. Those days he was searching for a larger company, asked me for advice and so I recommended The Royal Ballet to him. And he has never made me feel any sort of regret about it. Working with him in the Royal has always been a pleasure. In ballet class he works at a full pace, no matter how difficult his schedule during the day, keenly listening to the teacher's corrections. For me, Carlos Acosta is a human being, fully dedicated to ballet art, who has such a gift from God.'

The rest of Carlos' day is spent in rehearsing, costume fittings, general planning, massages and going to the gym to build up his muscles. 'I have to do thousands of push-ups to lift the girls easily,' the Cuban laughed. If there is a performance at night, then the principal dancers are free to go home and rest, returning to the theatre around two to three hours before the performance to do their hair, make-up and a warm-up. The curtain comes down around ten fifteen p.m. and after showering and changing, it's off home to sleep before the routine begins again the next day. Life in the Opera House is always busy.

In 2003, he took the role of Apollo in Balanchine's neoclassical and exquisitely elegant one-act ballet. In this work, Apollo instructs his three muses in their arts and finally leads them to Mount Parnassus. His muses were ballerinas Darcey Bussell, Marianela Nuñez and Mara Galeazzi. It was a splendid cast and Carlos, bare-chested and wearing only pristine white tights, looked godlike.

A role that suited Carlos' quicksilver technique was originally created by Frederick Ashton for Mikhail Baryshnikov in 1980, in celebration of the Queen Mother's eightieth birthday. Called *Rhapsody*, it is known as a test of survival for the dancer who is constantly on the move, racing on and off stage, jumping, turning, changing directions, all at the speed of light and done with a mercurial sense of fun and ease. Carlos danced this in a compelling and enjoyable way, leaving the audience breathless when the music finally stopped and the curtains fell as he ended centre stage with a whimsical shrug of the shoulders. (A fellow Cuban friend, Yosvani Ramos, who danced with English National Ballet before joining Australian Ballet summed up Carlos' skilled foot-work as 'a cross between Baryshnikov and footballer David Beckham, rolled into one.')

In 2004, Carlos made his debut with Paris Opera

Ballet, dancing in Nureyev's production of *Don Quixote* – the first Cuban male to be invited to dance with this prestigious company. He gave a scorching performance oozing Caribbean charm and won the audience over. 'I enjoyed it very much,' he reported in *Dance Europe* in February 2005 after he had been voted Dancer of the Year by the magazine's readers. 'It's a magnificent company, very classical and pure and I appreciated that very much. But it was also nerve-wracking to be a guest (with that company) as they don't invite that many. So you felt that all eyes were on you, judging you. But I went well-prepared, aiming to do my best – and I think I did.'

Carlos took the appointment of principal guest artist of The Royal Ballet during that same year, which has given him the freedom to forge out a career to dance as guest artist with other companies in full-length productions or in gala concerts. He travels the world to perform with top companies like the Paris Opera Ballet, the Mariinsky (Kirov) Ballet, the Bolshoi Ballet, Australian Ballet, and American Ballet Theatre where he has danced in their highly acclaimed spring seasons. Also in that year he made his outstanding debut back at the Royal Opera House in George Balanchine's *Prodigal Son* with the French superstar ballerina Sylvie Guillem as the Siren. Jeffery Taylor wrote: 'Carlos Acosta is astonishing in the title role of the stylised, primitive parable *Prodigal*

Son. He moves through the broad brush strokes of emotion as naturally as the breath he draws and in one of the best performances of his life, he is unravelled by Sylvie Guillem's Siren, stripped naked by the Drinking Companions and reveals the depth of man's basic need for love and forgiveness.'*

Carlos has danced regularly with Australian ballerina Leanne Benjamin during his career, and one of his most dramatic performances with her has been in Kenneth MacMillan's gruelling but gripping masterpiece *Mayerling*. The ballet tells the story of Crown Prince Rudolf's tragic and psychological descent into drug-induced degradation, ending with a joint suicide pact with his lover Mary Vetsera. It is one of those ballets that only succeeds when the main characters are utterly convincing for it is not a comfortable ballet to watch. For Carlos, there was much in the story of unhappiness, misunderstanding, loneliness that he could equate with and he gave the role of Rudolf much deep thought and energy. 'It is a role that is tough to dance all the way through,' he said. 'You have to pace yourself both in your physical and in your emotional output. You have to save enough energy for the final last moments of his life, so you have to know how to portion out your strength throughout the evening.'

---

* www.ballet.so.uk/Sunday Express website, 2 February 2004

A few years later at the 2006 International Festival of Ballet in Havana, Carlos was, as usual, one of the invited performers and always the public's favourite. They loved to shriek at his tricks and speed, and always eagerly awaited his performance, not sure what he was going to show them. This time they were in for a surprise! He had brought Leanne and Ricardo Cervera with him from The Royal Ballet to perform the final moments of *Mayerling*. It is a scene in which the tormented Crown Prince injects himself with morphine while he awaits his lover. She is brought to him by Bratfisch, his servant, who tries to lift the dark mood, a role neatly and strongly danced by Cervera. The audience remained numb in their seats, mesmerised by the black drama – their carefree Carlos, slumped in a chair, unrecognisable with his oiled hair and Clark Gable moustache. Now, rather than dazzle with leaps and turns, he roughly grabbed his lover and made passionate – and very graphic – love to her before their very eyes. The audience held its breath until the 'deed' was done and then, as the shock wore off, the auditorium reverberated with enthusiastic clapping and cheering. A few moments later though, they were back to the horrors of the story as the two committed suicide behind a screen – the gunshots making everyone in the theatre jump.

As Carlos has continued to charm balletomanes and

public alike, Monica Mason has no hesitation in singing Carlos' praises on his contribution to The Royal Ballet. 'Carlos has influenced the company with his fantastic work ethic – he studies hard every day and takes class with tremendous concentration. He never throws his weight around, never creates scenes and behaves brilliantly with his partners. He is a complete pleasure, is never moody, never complains and is appreciative of what we are doing. We have such respect for each other. The Royal Ballet has given him a real place in the ballet world. So many people have got to know him, to see him, and his guest contract with us has flown our flag around the world. He continues to be in this wonderful working relationship.'

10

A Cuban Tale for Everyone

'Tocororo mustn't be thought of as a masterpiece.
It was created simply for fun'

IT WAS IN 2002 and Carlos had been at The Royal
Ballet for four years when his career took a new and
bold turn. After Tiekka's departure, he had been constantly plagued with feelings of loneliness and with
his sadness came constant reminders of how much
he missed his home, the warm sunshine and the
energies and conviviality of the Cuban people. True,
he was gaining fame and followers whenever he set
foot on the stage, but in his time away from the theatre, he too often felt dejected, and longed for family
life and all the bustle and comfort it offered. He also
hungered after new challenges. He had danced most
of the big leading roles in the classical repertoire and,

while he loved creating roles in new works, these were few and far between. When he went to guest in other companies, everyone always wanted him to do the blockbuster tricks he was famous for and excelled in. While these trips made him money, he felt that he should push himself into pastures new. He needed more stimulation. If he was to keep progressing, he needed to find new projects to inspire him. So, during the empty hours when he was not in the busy studios among the other Royal dancers, he sowed the first seeds of a plan that would create a new facet in his life – he would make his first attempt to choreograph. It was a huge step to take and a thought that he tried to reject many times as inconceivable. What did he know about choreography, especially since he now was constantly dancing fantastic works by the greatest choreographers in the world? But the idea just kept returning. What should he do? He was not interested in creating another classical balletic *pas de deux* – he had danced enough of these. He wanted to bring something completely different and unusual to his audiences, something they had never seen him dance before. After much soul-searching, he made a decision. What better subject than his own culture? He could give a new view of his beloved country, one that the sun-worshipping, snorkelling tourists did not get to see on their package holidays to the golden beaches and turquoise seas of Cuba. It would be a celebration of his own Hispanic roots and show his homeland in a shining light of exuberant dances and brilliant dancers. What's more, he would spin his own autobiography into the production, so he could show the challenges, the initial loneliness of ballet, and the joy and friendship that he discovered when dancing with others. Yes, it would give Western audiences a taste of Caribbean life and bring an evening of that potent Cuban sunshine and exuberance into the very heart of London – and later, hopefully, to other cities. It was a wild card. Would audiences be satisfied with his first, possibly feeble, attempt at choreographing? Would he become the laughing-stock of the classical world? He had no need to worry. The public adored Carlos no matter what he did, and despite the naivety and simplicity of the scenario he eventually created, the production was to score a fantastic success.

Tocororo – A Cuban Tale was premiered in Havana on 15 February 2003 at the Gran Teatro de la Habana before President Fidel Castro and a theatre packed with a cheering audience. Then, five months later, it came to London where it also received a resounding reception.

The work's gestation period was complicated and often challenging, as Carlos still had to keep his contractual commitments and perform with various

companies. Always having danced just one established role in a production, he soon found how complicated it is to create a new work for many dancers
– especially with such a busy working schedule – and
to envision all the trappings that go into the final
staging. Then, and most importantly, there was the
money to be found to fund the project. Fortunately
for Carlos, a young Londoner named Andy Wood
came on the scene at the early stages of planning and
between them, they started to work on the development and financing of the show.

Andy Wood is the founder-director of ¡Como
No!, a company which promotes live Latin music
and has been bringing musicians and artists, many
from Cuba, over to Britain on tour since 1986. But
this was the first time he had to deal with a classical
ballet dancer.

'I first met Carlos in 1998,' he reminisced. 'I was
staging a benefit at the Royal Festival Hall on London's
South Bank to raise money for cultural programmes
in Cuba, and Carlos came as one of our guests. After
that evening, we would occasionally meet at different
functions, but it was not until the turn of the new
century that we started to discuss his idea for a show.'
When Carlos had initially laid plans for his production, he had contacted Alistair Spalding, then the
director of programming at Sadler's Wells Theatre in
Islington, who, after hearing Carlos' skeleton ideas,

suggested that he talk to Andy. So Carlos had immediately called the ¡Como No! office.

'We sat in a cafe and started discussing what he
had in mind,' continued Andy Wood. 'It was now
2000. We talked over his first ideas on creating a
show, what it would be, and what it would entail, and
I came up with a budget. Over the next two years
we sought ways of presenting it and of finding the
money.

'I had a contact in America named David Sefton
who had been appointed Director of UCLA Performing Arts where he directs an eclectic array of music,
dance and performance. He liked the ideas that Carlos had to offer and it became a pet project to see if he
could make it work. He was sure that he could obtain
the necessary money from the local Cuban com-
munity right there in southern California. But when
nothing immediately came of it there, we decided to
pitch the project in New York.' Carlos and Andy set
off for Manhattan to discuss their plans with potential new sponsors of the show. They congregated early
one morning in The Half-King, the cafe-bar owned
by Sebastian Junger, author of *The Perfect Storm*.
Wood remembers that Carlos was very animated and
enthusiastic, telling the punters all his plans, jumping up every other moment to show them the dancing he planned to include in his show. 'We both had
great hope after that meeting,' he reported. 'Then 9/11

happened and all funding dried up. The venues that were committed to dance projects suddenly disappeared.' The terrible terrorist attack on the Twin Towers in lower Manhattan changed the whole world, including the cultural scene in the United States. No one was now interested in funding a new dance programme. The young dancer from Cuba had to start looking elsewhere.

Wood returned to London and started pruning the budget. 'We decided to approach Alistair once more,' he said. 'He was now the chief executive and artistic director of Sadler's Wells, which was good news and was able to speculate the success for his theatre of a project that had Carlos Acosta's name on it, while I was ready to take the financial risk. Carlos had now decided to use Cuban contemporary dancers and this meant that we were locked into creating the work in Cuba. Communication with the island was still difficult and frustrating, but plans were laid for starting the work. It was decided to hold the premiere in Havana in February 2003, and then we would bring the show to London in July. Carlos in fact preferred this opportunity to produce the show in Cuba first, as he recognised the high risk of opening in London in front of a more sophisticated and critical audience. He then would have the five months between the performances to prune his work and make any adjustments needed.'

So, early in December 2002, Carlos started to work on the show, giving himself two and a half months to create his first-ever choreographic piece, which, as yet did not have a name. Wood was basically the producer in the economic sense of finding the money. The creative work and inspiration for sets, scenario, design and choreography was Carlos' responsibility. Part of Wood's job was to put a production team around Carlos and pay the team. That meant flying back and forth from London every two weeks with what he described as 'wodges of money stuffed in my pockets. Going through airport security was always interesting!' Looking back, Wood stated that though there were many incredible challenges to getting the project off the ground, he thought the hardest part of the production was 'organising the car'. Carlos had decided that he wanted a car in the show, one of those wonderful vintage cars that proudly prowl around the dusty streets of Cuba's capital in all their vibrant red, blue, green or yellow repainted glory. His eyes were set on one of these gas-guzzling 1950s American classics for his show – Chevrolets, Studebakers, Oldsmobiles – romantic relics of a past era, lovingly cared for and skilfully maintained. How to get hold of one was the problem Andy faced – but not for long. With his outstanding career both at home and abroad, Carlos has become an iconic figure in Cuba. He is now recognised all over the island, especially as he often appears on both of Cuba's television channels. With his charismatic character and ready smile, everyone wanted to help him. One day, he and Andy were driving along a street in Havana when he spotted a red Chevrolet. They followed it and flagged down its driver. Carlos quickly charmed its owner and negotiated to use the car on stage at the García Lorca for the show's performances. An agreement was made and two days before opening night, the car was delivered.

'The idea was that the car would come through the back doors of the theatre onto the stage. But no one took into account that the doors were six feet in the air! Here was one and a half tons of car to get from the street onto the stage,' remembers Andy. 'The Cuban carpenters set to and collected some driftwood and, with tiny bits of wood and nails, made a ramp up to the open doorway. My heart was in my mouth each time the car went on it. Would it hold the heavy car, and what about the dancers on stage and especially those inside the car if it dropped? There was always the worry, especially when one time it did actually roll back. No one in Cuba has any idea what insurance is. There is no risk assessment or insurance in the theatre there, so we prayed that everything would work out well each night. It was a heart-stopping moment every time it made its appearance up the ramp onto the stage.'

Andy Wood was also responsible for bringing out

from London all the materials, needles, threads and miscellaneous items for the costumes and it was a slow job getting them made. Carlos had to be patient. In London when he went for a fitting at The Royal Ballet, his costume was completed miraculously quickly. In Cuba the dancers had to wait for the dressmakers to find time between their regular work for the Ballet Nacional, and it was a long process. As well as conceiving the idea for the show, choreographing and rehearsing it, Carlos was 'hands on' in every area of the production – driving here to pick up something, meeting with set workers to make sure instructions were being carried out, working with individual dancers and keeping his own technique at peak level as he was not only dancing in the show, but had to keep popping off to fulfil guest contracts with classical ballet companies outside of Cuba. The work was hard and relentless and Wood, who optimistically packed his swimming trunks on each visit, never got to use them. But gradually everything came together.

Carlos decided to give his dance-ballet the name of *Tocororo*, after the colourful national bird of Cuba. He worked hard on his creation, not wanting, or expecting it to be seen as a stunning masterpiece, but as general entertainment, something unexpected and fun, and most importantly, a joyful evening out. The two-act production fused together the art of classical ballet with breakdancing, salsa and street dancing, along with the rhythms and dances of Cuba, all wrapped up loosely in his autobiographical storyline. He felt he owed a huge debt to his mother country and this was one way of repaying it.

The story of *Tocororo* unfolds with a young country boy in a white shirt with rolled-up sleeves, tattered jeans and a straw hat, setting off for the big city to seek his fortune. As in Carlos' own life, the aged father chides the boy for his reluctance to leave home. Alone in the big city he studies ballet for several years but remains a loner. Seeing others joyfully dancing on the streets, he tries to join them and meets up with the Moor, the local cigar-smoking gang leader who mocks him for his pristine technique. But soon the young boy has learned, and even bettered, the loose-limbed dancing of the mobster and is accepted whole-heartedly by everyone. The simplicity of the tale was in sharp contrast to the intensity of the dancing with its hip-wiggling, toe-tapping music from the on-stage band.

Carlos used dancers from Danza Contemporánea de Cuba, and their energetic and exuberant dancing made the perfect backdrop to his own performing of both classical and Cuban styles. He was careful, however, to make sure that there was plenty of vibrant choreography for everyone and not to make *Tocororo* look as though it was an ego trip, created to display his own talents. To portray himself as a young boy,

Carlos looked no further than to his own nephew – his sister Marilin's son. At thirteen, Yonah Acosta was the perfect mould for the role. 'He's like a son to me,' said the proud uncle. 'I really believe he will do well. He reminds me of myself though he hasn't had the same challenges. Yonah has the physique, the looks and the talent to become a great dancer.' At this time Yonah was still training at the National School of Ballet under Ramona de Saá's keen guidance. Coltish with long slim limbs, he was very professional in his first big stage performance and made the ideal child-hero of the story, However it was sometimes hard for the young teenager to work in that intense, specialised atmosphere and often be pushed beyond his normal limits. But, like his uncle, he succeeded with flying colours. There was a touching moment in the scenario when the two Acostas mirror-imaged each other in steps, costume and ability as childhood gives way to adolescence. Alexander Varona performed the Moor with impeccable action, and for the love interest, Carlos invited Veronica Corveas, a member of Ballet Nacional de Cuba.

Finally the day dawned for the premiere and while Carlos had sent a personal invitation to President Fidel Castro to attend the performance, it was only in the late afternoon that it became evident that he was actually going to come. Police arrived en masse and moved all cars from the street in front of the theatre and secret service personnel checked out the inside of the auditorium. Alistair Spalding had flown over for the premiere and was duly impressed with Castro's presence at *Tocororo*. 'I arrived at the theatre for the show,' he related with a grin, 'and was surprised that, when I entered the auditorium, everyone stood up. For me? I wondered. I then saw Fidel Castro had come in. I was sitting just a few seats away from him.' Chery, Carlos' mentor, sat beside the President since Madame Alonso did not attend. Alistair confirmed what several people reported: that the President talked loudly throughout the performance, presumably in appreciation, and when the final curtain had fallen to thunderous cheering and applauding, he had gone on stage to congratulate the dancers and musicians, and had stayed talking for nearly two hours. No one could leave until he had finished!

After a night of celebration, Carlos, never one to rest on his laurels, was up early for a meeting with Spalding. It was obvious that the piece needed some clever editing for London audiences. But Carlos now had confidence in the work's success. For Spalding, it was the dancer's magnetic cheerful personality and joy-filled production that forecast that the London shows would be a sell-out. And they were.

When the news quickly travelled that *Tocororo* with Carlos dancing in it was coming to London, the box-office buzzed with activity. Ismene Brown, dance critic of the *Daily Telegraph*, wrote: 'Beg, blag or bribe a ticket, but move very fast. Even those who have never come near classical ballet, and to whom the name Carlos Acosta means nothing, will be excited and moved by *Tocororo*. Only a man of magnetic talent and burning integrity could make a show about Cuba's sizzling dance styles that's also an intense personal drama about the complications of being super-gifted.'*

Given that *Tocororo* was the creation of a novice choreographer, it still captured the viewer with its vibrancy and enthusiasm. The atmosphere at Sadler's Wells on the opening night of a two-week run was one of festive anticipation, and when the lights finally dimmed and the live band ambled onto a brightly lit stage and started to beat out percussive rhythms, everyone settled down in this carnival atmosphere to see what the young man had achieved in his first full work for the stage. While delighted by the response *Tocororo* received, Carlos' greatest joy was that his whole family flew over to London to attend the premiere.

Tocororo had two sell-out seasons in London, and toured to Hong Kong, Austria, Italy and Turkey. It returned to UK stages in a forty-minute distillation

---

* *Daily Telegraph*, 17 July 2003

of the full work in one of Carlos' other ballet-evening presentations. While *Tocororo* was a huge toe-tapping success with audiences everywhere, it more importantly proved to Carlos himself that he had more than classical wizardry to offer the public. This experience gave him something to build on as the end of his classical dancing days loomed ever nearer.

11

The Role He Was Born to Dance

'This must have been the reason I became a dancer'

BY 2007, CARLOS had been with The Royal Ballet for nine years and was regularly demonstrating his prowess technically and artistically in most of the important roles in its repertoire. He had danced everything from prince to prodigal son, but he was always ready for a challenge. Then along came *Spartacus* with the greatest heroic male dance role in the ballet world's repertoire. And Carlos' incredible talents met all of that role's demanding criteria.

'I wanted to dance *Spartacus* before I retired from dancing,' he said. 'It may be a young man's role because of the stamina and the athleticism that it requires, but it also needs the emotion and dramatic input that a more mature dancer can bring from life experiences.

And I certainly have these in abundance. I felt this ballet would be the pinnacle of my career.'

The highly charged three-act ballet is one of the Bolshoi Ballet's most famous signature works of the twentieth century. Set in the first century BC, a time when the Romans held control of a large expanding empire, the ballet depicts the struggle for freedom by the common man against oppression. It relates the fate of the Thracian slave Spartacus, captured with his people by Crassus, the cruel and decadent general of the Roman army who takes the shackled captives to Rome to be sold as slaves. Chosen to be a gladiator, Spartacus is forced to kill a fellow slave in a blindfolded duel for the amusement of Crassus and his friends at an orgy. Filled with remorse, he vows to escape and free his people.

The ballet recounts the struggles he faces and the battles he must fight in the cause of freedom. The ballet is inventively constructed, offering contrasting scenes of blazing action and poignant monologues in which Spartacus reveals his innermost thoughts. There are also lyrical and romantic duets between Spartacus and his wife Phrygia, all danced to the stirring score by Aram Khachaturian, a Soviet composer of Armenian descent. This epic work, created by the Bolshoi's director and chief choreographer Yuri Grigorovich in 1968 at the height of the cold war, exudes all the elements of Soviet ideology and symbolism:

power, sacrifice, the underdog fighting against the tyranny of decadent, imperialistic powers, sacrifice rather than dishonour. In creating his masterpiece, Grigorovich disregarded the traditional concept of classical ballet where the ballerina is the focal point, to put the spotlight on the men. His Spartacus shows off the Bolshoi's vast quantity of virile male dancers (the envy of every Western ballet company) who powerfully pour across the stage with larger-than-life fervour.

The role of the slave leader Spartacus is more than just another ballet role to be learned, rehearsed and then danced. It requires the strength of an elephant, the power of a tiger, the agility of a mountain goat, the constitution of a bear, and the speed and grace of a cheetah. It demands some of the most incredibly difficult but awe-inspiring dynamic movements in the ballet repertoire, plus non-stopping physical force and bravura from its hero throughout the ballet. Spartacus must inspire his fellow slaves to follow him, and he does this with heart-stopping leaps, turns and jumps, as well as with the sincerity of his acting.

Any previous dancers of the role will tell you that it is a 'killer' – each performance leaving them emotionally drained and physically exhausted. Because of the sheer strain and effort required, those dancing Spartacus usually find themselves physically lighter by around three kilos at the end of each performance. So, in order to stay the course and exude the same amount of energy at the finale as at the opening leap, great physical and mental preparation must be done – in the gym as well as the ballet studio.

Spartacus is one of those fabulous roles that can make heroes of those who meet its challenges – off stage as well as in the theatre. So it was not surprising that the ballet made household names of its earliest exponents in 1968. Creating the role of Spartacus at the ballet's premiere was Vladimir Vasiliev who, with physical prowess and natural good looks, gave a breath-taking interpretation, conveying compassion, resolve and sensitivity. The second Spartacus was Mikhail Lavrovsky who was equally compelling and presented a deeply thought-out and more passionate character. The next generation found thrills in the Tatar dancer Irek Mukhamedov, whose wonderful charismatic personality charmed both on stage and off as he, seemingly effortlessly, whizzed through the challenging choreography, showing spectacular new trick endings to his leaps. Today's Bolshoi has a new superhero who made his Spartacus debut on tour in Amsterdam in 2008 when he was nineteen years old. Ivan Vasiliev (no relation to Vladimir) offers a youthful, energetic leader who inspires fellow slaves to revolt by his fervour and persuasion, and by his rocket-propelled leaps and complicated turns.

And then there is Carlos who had to step into the canvas ballet shoes of the role knowing he had both history and competition to face up to, especially being only the second non-Russian dancer to be invited to perform this ballet with the great company – (Nicolas Le Riche from Paris Opera Ballet danced the role at the Bolshoi Theatre in 1994). The idea and invitation for Carlos to come to the hallowed halls of this famous theatre and dance the fabled role came because of his reputation for excellence, and first-hand observation of his dedication and willingness to try new things, and was instigated by Boris Akimov.

For several years, Boris Akimov has been one of the regular guest teachers invited by Monica Mason to give class at The Royal Ballet. A member of the Bolshoi Ballet since 1965, Akimov has been widely recognised as a brilliant dancer and teacher. Since stepping down from performing he has not only taught class and supervised rehearsals at the Bolshoi Theatre but he has been a popular and much loved teacher in international ballet companies in Japan, Denmark, Holland, Austria, Germany, Italy and England. His classes are renowned for the emphasis he places on carefully and slowly warming up the dancer's body, and the graduating step-by-step exercises he gives to strengthen muscles, technique and style. For many years, Akimov has come to London for two to three weeks at the beginning of January to teach in one of the big airy studios high up in the renovated backstage area of the Royal Opera House. And it was there that he got to know and admire Carlos as a dancer.

In 2000, Akimov was appointed artistic director of the Bolshoi Ballet, a position that he took on with great dedication and deliberation. During his short tenure in the job, he was instrumental in organising the staging of several Western ballets new to the Russian public. He is renowned for his friendliness, charm and kindness and it is these qualities that have made him many friends over the years in all the different companies in which he has taught, and with the people with whom he has come into contact. It had been on one of his visits to London that Akimov, still artistic director of the Bolshoi Ballet, first thought of Carlos as Spartacus. 'It was in a discussion with some friends that the idea came up. I was immediately excited about the prospect. I knew from watching him in my classes how dedicated he was to his work and how much he relished new opportunities to develop more skills. When I next saw Carlos, I asked him about the idea, and he was very enthusiastic about it,' said Akimov. 'I reported the idea to the general director of the Bolshoi Theatre, Anatoly Iksanov, who said it would "probably be a possibility". Yuri Grigorovich, choreographer of the ballet, gave his blessing to the idea also. So I set the wheels in motion to invite Carlos to come to Moscow to learn and perform the leading role of Spartacus.' It was an inspired decision, and a project that would bring acclaim to both the Bolshoi company and to Carlos, who was eager to take up the offer, knowing full well the enormous challenge – and not just the physical one – that lay before him.

When the official permission came, Carlos received a DVD of the ballet from the company and set about teaching himself the initial steps and learning the ballet's structure. Carlos soon realised that this was no ordinary role and that he would need extra time to prepare his body for it and he began to work on the steps whenever he was not performing or preparing other productions. 'Then I found space in my schedule – a month, rather than the six weeks recommended,' he reported. By this time there was another artistic director in charge of the Bolshoi Ballet, a young Ukrainian-born, internationally recognised dancer and choreographer, Alexei Ratmansky. Fortunately he thoroughly approved of the idea of Carlos dancing Spartacus and a new date was set. So, after his regular day's work, Carlos would return to The Royal Ballet studios to teach himself the outlines of the role from the DVD, aided by Alexander Agadzhanov, a former Russian dancer who has been coaching the principal dancers of The Royal Ballet for many years. With his constantly busy schedule, Carlos admitted that it was very hard to find the time and energy for the necessary preparation for his *Spartacus* debut. 'It was not like I was going to dance something familiar like *Don Quixote* or *Swan Lake*,' he said. 'Every company has those ballets and I already know my roles in them. No, here was a raw, new adventure for me. I needed five to six weeks to learn the ballet in order to dance it properly. I had to get used to the musical score as well as the choreography, and I also had to build up my muscular strength. The Bolshoi is famous for this *Spartacus*. It is a legendary ballet, one I had heard about in my school days back in Cuba, but had never seen. And I really wanted to dance it before I retired from my dancing career. It is very rare to find a ballet today that demands so much continuous action from the male dancer and *Spartacus* was this one. The ballet is full of emotion and challenge, so I knew I had to dance it – especially since it has all the elements of my own life in it: the struggle of minorities, passion, and a desire to break free from the mould. The time was right physically for me to do it. Now I had to find time in my calendar to make it happen.' When that gap appeared, he was off.

A month before his June 2007 debut, Carlos set off for Russia again, this time on his own and with more important work to do than just a gala *pas de deux*.

The famed columned Bolshoi Theatre in Theatre Square was wrapped in plastic as it underwent a long and much needed *kapitalny remont* – complete restoration. During this disruption all opera and ballet performances were held in the New Theatre building situated right next door on what used to be the old parking lot. Smaller than the Bolshoi, the New Theatre, or Filial, combines modern comfort with elegant charm. Now with the news of Carlos' arrival, the backstage area fluttered with excitement. Everyone wanted to watch him in class and in rehearsals. Fortunately for the young Cuban, Boris Akimov was still working at the Bolshoi despite no longer holding the reins of the company. He had returned to his first love – that of teaching and of handing down his extensive knowledge of the Bolshoi's repertoire, especially the works that he had danced during his lifetime. So Carlos was happy to see his familiar and friendly face again and partake of his first-class teaching. Akimov had danced the other principal role in *Spartacus,* that of the malicious Crassus, a role which also demands vigorous action with a lot of jumping and strong acting skills. Now together with Mikhail Lavrovsky, who had been a superb Spartacus, they worked with Carlos each day in the Bolshoi studios, polishing and refining the steps the Cuban dancer had taught himself from the video.

The premiere was an absolute success. Ballerina

Nina Kaptsova who was later to partner Carlos when the Bolshoi performed *Spartacus* in Paris in 2008, remembers that both the Bolshoi company members and the audience were astonished by him. 'They wanted to see everything that he did. In stage rehearsals and his performances, everyone in the theatre, from coaches to costume fitters, filled the wings just to get a glimpse of him – making it hard for the dancers to get on and off stage. He didn't hold anything back but gave everything of himself. Just watching him when he was on stage pushed the entire company, from principals to corps de ballet, to exert themselves and give of their very best. Everyone, including me, fell in love with him!'

Despite the fact that dance styles have changed over the years with technique becoming more precise and refined, Carlos' schooling in Cuba had made him aware of the highly dramatic and expansive action of Soviet training and had given him an understanding of such propaganda-filled ballets as *Spartacus*. The ostentatious physicality and shrewd dogma demonstrated in the choreography was very much a part of that now-past Soviet era. And it is a structure that many Western critics today find excessive and stylised. Yet, while the political system has changed in Russia, there is no denying that Grigorovich's genius in the taut construction and action-packed work still serves as a vehicle for the talents of the younger male dance generation, and thus remains a significant part of the Bolshoi Ballet's repertoire and history. The ballet also demands more than just physical power. It must be convincing dramatically.

Over the years, Carlos had turned into a deep thinker and now he delved into the character of Spartacus. Always an individualist, he was determined to make it his own. He believed that the role was tailor-made for him and so he embedded into it elements from his own personal life experiences. Together with the big dancing needed to demonstrate the character's power, these individual prerequisites showed that the ballet was the perfect vehicle for him. And he succeeded in it brilliantly. Acosta imprinted his hero with humanity, humility, and a zeal for the cause of freedom. He threw himself into the drama, convincing the critics with his innermost passions. His two performances in Moscow were a triumph. Much to everyone's delight, Acosta had taken up the challenge and had proved that he was truly worthy of joining the other Bolshoi legends in this role.

A month after his outstanding debut at the Bolshoi Theatre, the Russian company came to Carlos' own stomping ground, London, for a three-week tour at the London Coliseum. Among the full-length ballets they brought was *Spartacus*. The news that Carlos would dance the ballet just twice for London audiences set the theatre's cash registers ringing. Tickets for his two shows were the hottest items around that summer, and sold out immediately. The buzz from fans and media alike was electric. On the evening of 6 August 2007, the house was packed – and the queue of hopefuls who waited for any returned tickets was long, winding around the box office area. The audience inside waited in great anticipation. The curtain rose and a harsh spotlight fell on the arrogant face of Crassus, then gradually panned to show him standing astride his chariot as his soldiers triumphantly goose-stepped around him. When they exited, the stage darkened and a group of slaves huddled together. Suddenly one of the slaves slowly stood upright, and the power of defiance rather than defeat that he expressed sent chills throughout the auditorium. This simple gesture and the expression on Carlos' face as he stood there – not a step had been danced as yet – confirmed that here was a true heir to this great masculine role. Needless to say, as the story unfolded and as the hero showed off his amazing physical abilities, the ballet continued to astound. The whole company rose to the occasion with each dancer offering one hundred per cent in effort and conviction throughout the evening. Spurred on by the Cuban missile in their midst, the other principals delivered convincing acting and incredible dancing, while the Bolshoi's own orchestra surged passionately with Khachaturian's score. The evening was rapturously received and he

178

won outstanding reviews for his performance: 'Power and drama surge through his very being, igniting every aspect of his performance. Slicing the air in the repetitive diagonal *jetés*, he barely touched the floor before becoming airborne again like a smooth stone skimming the surface of a placid lake. Other times, his sheer force exploded in barrel-turns ending with a knife-cutting double that had the audience gasping, then cheering. Alternating with this turbo drive were the tender, intimate moments with wife Phrygia (the soft and lyrical Anna Antonicheva), and the dizzying one-handed high lifts which he accomplished with assurance.'* The ballet world had a new slave hero to marvel at.

Early in January 2008, the Bolshoi Ballet went on tour to Paris taking *Spartacus* for the first time to the French capital. Carlos had been invited back to dance the role and this time his performance was to be filmed.

In the oval Petipa studio at the very top of the Paris Opera building, Carlos and his new Phrygia, Nina Kaptsova, rehearsed under the watchful eye of Mikhail Lavrovsky. Carlos, wearing his favourite baggy, bibbed woollen warmer over his dance clothes was eager and receptive to all of Lavrovsky's coaching. The senior dancer shed his years as he relived

---

* *Dance Magazine.* October 2007

some of the role's greatest moments, miraculously recalling every tiny detail and demonstrating the finer points of the role to his eager and receptive pupil. With just one week to refine and remember the nuances, and practise their partnering skills, the two dancers used every precious moment they were allowed in the studio. As they worked hard that first morning in the upper room, each facet of the leading role was visibly polished until it sparkled. Carlos' earlier encounter with the ballet had been miraculous in his ability to learn just the steps and the actions in such a short time – and he had proved that when he had performed successfully both in Moscow and London. But now, ever the perfectionist, he was making sure that he incorporated every tenor and finely tuned choreographic and dramatic detail into this performance, especially since the ballet was being filmed for posterity at its Paris premiere. Fortunately he was again in Lavrovsky's excellent hands for this momentous moment. When the young man did not get a timing right, or turned the wrong way during a rehearsal, Lavrovsky was up on his feet showing, with all the passion of his 1970s performances, how to do the step correctly. This was the kind of coaching that Carlos had received in Cuba – the originator of the role passing down their first-hand knowledge to the next generation.

Mikhail Lavrovsky, born in Tbilisi, Georgia in

1941, has an impeccable ballet pedigree. His father Leonid was the renowned director of the Bolshoi Ballet in Moscow, and is recognised as one of the Soviet Union's greatest choreographers whose dramatic masterpieces, such as his epic *Romeo and Juliet*, influenced the style and development of Russian ballet. Mikhail's mother Elena Chikvaidze was a ballerina with the Bolshoi Ballet for thirteen years before becoming a teacher at the Bolshoi School, consequently the young Mikhail was brought up in the Bolshoi's studios watching his parents at work. He later trained at the Bolshoi School and became a member of the company in 1961. Perceptive and cultured in all forms of art with an enquiring and open mind, Lavrovsky has always been willing to share his extensive knowledge with young eager dancers. Enter Carlos Acosta. The two made a perfect match and Lavrovsky, using his own experiences of the role as taught to him by Yuri Grigorovich, was very happy to hand down the red mantle of Spartacus onto such worthy shoulders. It was now Carlos' turn to take on the legendary role. Mikhail, or 'Misha', not only called him 'my artistic son', but also 'my spiritual son' as he felt they were closely knit both spiritually and in their mutual desire for perfection. He recognised the young Cuban's great theatrical output and his ability to retain the intensity of the character right up to the very end. There was never a single moment when the drama relaxed. On the day of Carlos' premiere in Paris, Lavrovsky went to the Russian Orthodox Church in Paris and prayed to God 'to put this boy in Your Hands tonight'. The prayer obviously worked.

Nina Kaptsova had been astonished when director Alexei Ratmansky told her she would be partnering Carlos in Paris. She had seen him when he was dancing at the Bolshoi but, until their first encounter in the Paris studio, had not spoken to him. The petite, delicate-looking Nina has been steadily climbing the ranks of the Bolshoi Ballet. Her dancing is sublimely lyrical with beautiful arm and leg movements that cut strong yet ethereal swathes in the air. She is light and pliable and makes every step look graceful and easy. But most of all she has an incredible intensity in her acting and completely gives herself to her roles. Her slight build, wide-eyed expressive face and seeming vulnerability made her the perfect Phrygia to Carlos' sturdy Spartacus. And she spoke of her utter surprise when she was cast with him.

'I had first seen Carlos when he came to dance *Don Quixote* at a gala in Moscow a while back, so of course I knew who he was and his standing as an international star. And though Phrygia is one of the roles that I dance, I expected Anna (Antonicheva) would be his partner again on tour in Paris. I never dreamed that I would ever get to dance with him and couldn't believe it when Ratmansky told me. Because I had never partnered him, I was very concerned about the technical aspect of it. There was so little time for us to rehearse together to get the difficult *pas de deux* and lifts secure, especially since our first performance was to be filmed. But as soon as we started our rehearsal, I felt that we were going to be all right. Right away I felt the details, the emotional approach to each other, and it was wonderful to dance together as if with "one breath". Carlos dances with such power and emotion even in the studio and it was so easy to show passion to him – even with my husband watching! [Nina's husband is Alexei Melentiev, a company pianist who was naturally present at every studio rehearsal.] The most important thing is to feel that Spartacus is a real man – the more manly he is, the softer Phrygia has to be. And we felt we expressed this. This ballet experience has easily been one of the high moments of my artistic life so far.' At the time, Nina was twenty-five years old.

The magic was woven right there in a rehearsal room in the Paris Opera House – the expertise of an earlier generation being placed on the shoulders of a new artist. 'It's a privilege to work with Carlos,' said Lavrovsky. 'He is a deep thinker and ready to learn everything he can. He's like a sponge, sucking up everything that's shown to him. And he will try and try again until it is perfect. He is doing it for his art and not for himself and I admire him for that.' Carlos responded with: '*Spartacus* brings all the elements of my life, my childhood, my dancing together. It's been amazing to learn and dance.'

Every challenge that cropped up was deftly handled – especially that of language. Both Lavrovsky and Acosta started with very basic English but to convey nuances of interpretation and technique, more specific information was needed. And the answer was there in the person of Olga Smoak who had also come to Paris to see Carlos dance Spartacus. She had known Lavrovsky personally for many years and Acosta from his first steps outside Cuba and from the festivals in Moscow, so immediately, with the two men's blessings and gratitude, she began to translate from Spanish into Russian and back again, throwing in French when anyone from Paris Opera popped in to watch. It was an answer to the prayers of the two dancers and their mentor as time was very precious. The first rehearsal now proceeded smoothly and quickly, and the requisite lustre soon began to show on Carlos' interpretation and actions.

On 22 January, at the Opera National de Paris, Palais Garnier, with cameras at the ready and the French audience anticipating, *Spartacus* took off. A proud Lavrovsky stayed in the wings offering reassurance and giving last-minute tips to his star pupil whenever he came off stage. 'Man, when you are in the wings, you do a lot of puffing and panting in this ballet,' remembers Carlos. The performance was rapturously received by the French audience, and Carlos was applauded by the whole company and kissed by the choreographer, Yuri Grigorovich, who saw him dance the high-powered role in his ballet for the first time that evening. The renowned choreographer and ex-director of the Bolshoi Ballet seemed very happy with the evening. Lavrovsky commented, 'At first I was stunned by Carlos' performance and then I was thrilled – thrilled that he took everything I gave him and made it his own.'

For the exhausted but supremely happy Carlos, it had been a fantastic evening and he reiterated his joy about having been given the opportunity and honour to perform this role. 'I know that all my life I have been preparing for this role, it was waiting for me to claim it and I finally realise why I was destined to learn to dance. Thank God that I had the opportunity. I feel fulfilled as a dancer now.'

12

Sharing His Present with His Past

'Cubans will never forget it'

IT WAS A HOT MUGGY MORNING in 2008 and festival time again in Havana. Morning class had just ended and the dancers glistened with sweat. The torrential tropical downpours of the early morning, combined with the heat of the now high November sun, provided a sauna-like atmosphere in the studio. For the dancers of the Ballet Nacional de Cuba it was a normal and natural temperature for their strenuous exercises. But for the visiting guest performers from Russia, the UK and Europe, it was hot, hard work and their bodies glistened.

Watching the class were two representatives of The Royal Ballet – Kevin O'Hare, the company manager, and Anthony Russell Roberts who, at that time, was the administrative director. They were in Havana, not to attend the festival but to sort out the possibilities of bringing the British ballet company on tour to Cuba. Their somewhat secretive mission paid off, for six months later in May, The Royal Ballet issued a press release entitled 'Royal Ballet to make historic first trip to Cuba, July 14–18, 2009'.

Carlos, who has remained loyal to his native company, continuing to dance with them whenever his schedule allows, had been the main instigator between the two companies in organising the momentous trip, which had taken over two years of negotiating. It was a plan he dearly wanted to succeed. He wanted his people to see the British company he had been dancing with for the past eleven years, and to introduce them to works and styles that they had never seen before. The visit would also demonstrate to them that his great sacrifice of leaving home and country had ultimately been worth it, as he had been able to continuously develop his unique talent. But most importantly of all, he wanted them to realise that whenever and wherever he danced around the world, he was flying the flag of Cuba's great dance training.

Carlos stated that The Royal Ballet's visit to his homeland was possibly the most important ballet event in Cuba in the fifty years since Fidel Castro's revolution. Indeed it had been three decades since the country had seen its last full overseas company – Russia's Bolshoi Ballet – on tour at a time when the two countries were friendly with each other. This first visit to the communist island by an international ballet company of such high repute as The Royal Ballet was a tremendous cultural coup for both countries. It was not expected to be, and never was, a money-making venture for the British company. While the Cubans covered all local expenses, the short trip cost The Royal Ballet over one million pounds. But it was money they felt was well spent.

In July 2009, nearly one hundred dancers and backstage crew set off for the small Caribbean island. The repertoire they took for their five performances consisted of one full-length ballet, two one-act works and a plethora of show-stopping gala pieces.

As soon as the news of the visit was announced, Cubans formed queues around the box office and all tickets – most of them costing less than the equivalent of one dollar – were sold out in no time at all. Because the occasion was such a big event and there were so many people who had been unable to obtain tickets, it was decided to erect huge screens on the steps of El Capitolio, the domed building which had been the seat of legislature in pre-revolution days, so that the general public could watch.

As on any big overseas tour, there were challenges to be overcome, but here in Cuba, even more than usual. The British technical crew knew that the country was prone to power cuts and brought their complete lighting needs with them, plus, fortunately, a generator which had to be used one night. Vinyl flooring had to be laid – British dancers are not used to performing on wooden floors, especially those that are rough and uneven. For The Royal Ballet's conductor Martin Yates, the challenge was in bringing the Cuban National Symphony up to scratch. Due to the strapped economic situation in the country, the orchestra had been downsized and many of the musicians had found other jobs. They were quickly rounded up and returned with enthusiasm and energy, and soon, under maestro Yates' baton, reached an acceptable standard. Then there were the British dancers. Not only did they have to cope with the ninety-degree heat and humidity, but five members of the company arrived with symptoms of the swine flu virus and were immediately put into quarantine by the Cubans. The casting lists had to be amended quickly and as if this was not enough to re-organise, principal dancer Rupert Pennefather was unable to take the leading role in Ashton's beautiful cameo one-act ballet, *A Month in the Country*. A message was speedily dispatched to London and Jonathon Cope was brought out of retirement to dance the role of the tutor Beliaev. The fact that he had not danced for several years – he is now a coach at The

Royal Ballet – did not deter him from performing the role and proving that he could still dance very well.

For the first three performances, the company danced in the stately, old-fashioned Gran Teatro de la Habana; while the two performances of Kenneth MacMillan's full-length ballet, *Manon*, were staged at the 5,000-seat Karl Marx Theatre. Those members of the public without tickets, from taxi drivers to barbers to shop assistants, sat in the warm evening air on the steps of El Capitolio.

The exorbitant costs of staging foreign productions has long been the thorn in the flesh of the Ballet Nacional, cutting them off from the development of techniques and styles, and from experiencing and seeing the rapid progress that classical ballet has made in the past forty years. One work typical of such advances in Western contemporary choreography was the very first ballet that The Royal Ballet performed, though at first it was met with silence. *Chroma*, the award-winning piece created in 2006 by Wayne McGregor, the company's resident choreographer, shows a hyper-articulated style of choreography with a sharp cutting edge, and it has the dancers turning themselves inside out in highly complicated gymnastic moves, while still retaining the technicalities of classical ballet. Gone are the sumptuous costumes and sets, and the heart-stirring music that the Cubans are used to. Instead, the dancers are confined in a box-like set, wear skimpy practice clothes and perform to a grinding beat. But now, as dancers started to contort and shape their super-strung lithe bodies to the non-stop pace demanded, the audience suddenly awakened to this revolutionary new style and showed their appreciation.

In sharp contrast, Ashton's *A Month in the Country,* which is danced to romantic strains of Chopin preludes, fulfilled the Cubans' expectations of a ballet, by offering a story set in pre-revolutionary Russia, with pretty costumes and elegant sets. However, the choreography often showed very different patterns to those that they were used to – the great English choreographer was known for filigree detailing of steps and sudden turns in unexpected directions, while the Cubans have tended to remain faithful to the flamboyant heroic style of the Russian technique. But they obviously liked the tasteful elegance of *Month* and clapped enthusiastically. Then another interval, and still there had been no sign of their much-loved Carlos – he was to appear in the divertissements coming up next.

Divertissements are always a popular part of a ballet evening. Here, dancers perform well-known highlights from classical ballets and they offer the viewers the chance to see the different dancers' technique, stamina and daring. The Cubans are excellent at this, showing off in multiple turns, speedy movements and balances that go on forever. So the gauntlet was down for the Royal dancers to prove that they too could be flashy and just as exciting. But there was a surprise. Two of the Ballet Nacional de Cuba's top dancers were to partner two from The Royal Ballet. First up was the *pas de deux* from *Don Quixote*, a showy piece beloved by dancers in competitions and in such divertissement programmes. The two dancers were the Royal's glorious ballerina Tamara Rojo partnered by Cuban Joel Carreño, the half-brother of Jose Manuel Carreño with whom the then eighteen-year-old Carlos had lived when in London with English National Ballet. However, at the last moment, it was touch-and-go as to whether this *pas de deux* would actually happen. Joel had been away on tour and returned only hours before the performance. This left the duo little time for the needed rehearsal especially since they had never danced with each other before. But it certainly didn't show in the performance. The two were brilliant: Joel leapt high and turned with panache and obvious fun, while Tamara showed she could balance and turn like a Cuban. She did triple *fouettés* and balanced on *pointe* in attitude with her leg held behind her for what seemed an age. The audience screamed with excitement. Next it was the reverse of roles: the Royal's Thiago Soares partnered the darling of the Ballet Nacional, Viengsay Valdés. This brilliant ballerina, whose balletic pyrotechnics have made her a household name in her own country, bewitched her Prince (Thiago) in the *Black Swan pas de deux*, showing off her own flamboyant *fouettés* and getting the Cubans to clap in time to the music. Other members of The Royal Ballet performed their duets and were well received, but the audience had thoughts of only one person that night, and everyone was anticipating him.

And finally the wait was over, and it was time for Cuba's favourite son to make an appearance. He was performing the popular and spectacular *pas de deux* from *Le Corsaire* with Tamara Rojo – the ballet about pirates, slaves and kidnapped harem girls. As the music began, Carlos, in gold lamé bolero and blue ballooning trousers, his arms on his shoulders and a plume in his headdress, leapt on stage, smiling, and fell to his knees in reverence, anticipating his ballerina. The crowds went wild and cheered so loudly that he found it hard to hear the music. As he slowly rose from his knees, Tamara entered from the opposite diagonal, regal in a striking blue tutu and tiara. She *bouréed* on *pointe* taking tiny steps that made her look as though she was gliding on ice. Her movements were incredibly neat and perfectly placed and she oozed refinement and dignity. Then the two of them started to show what they could do – Tamara stunned with fantastic triple pirouettes again, Carlos with double barrel turns and leaps that held him in the air. The audience started cheering and did not stop until the final moments when they all rose from their seats, before the music had even stopped playing, in a standing ovation. And it was not only in the theatre. On the street outside, the people sitting on the steps all joined in the jubilation.

After this final performance of the evening, all the dancers came on stage to take their bows. Suddenly Carlos and Joel left the stage, to return a few moments later bringing on the founder of Cuban ballet, Alicia Alonso. Dressed in sparkling turquoise, with matching trademark bandana, she joined the British dancers for their bows. Now totally blind, she needed the two men to guide her. As they held her tightly on each side they told her that Dame Monica Mason had come on stage and was presenting her with a bouquet of flowers and curtseying low in reverence for all that this remarkable Cuban woman has done for ballet in her country. The curtains finally closed and the theatre audience started to leave. But the dancers did not go straight to their dressing rooms. In full costume and make-up, they got on a bus and drove the short distance to El Capitolio where they surprised the 3,000-strong audience by going up onto a little stage and taking their final bows. The crowds were thrilled to see them in real life and everyone wanted to shake Carlos' hand. It truly was a memorable evening for so many: for the Cubans who had never seen these interesting productions before and also to have their beloved Carlos back on home territory, and for The Royal Ballet dancers who had never been received with such vocal enthusiasm and genuine delight as they had here in Havana. The crowds greeted Carlos like a hero. He grabbed a microphone and told them that the evening had been one of those moments in their lives that they would remember always. It would be one of those unforgettable occasions that they could tell their children and their grandchildren: 'We were there that evening when …' He noted that the amazing reception they had shown to ballet and to the dancers that evening was comparable to the same enthusiasm that is normally found with crowds at world-class football games. 'It was just amazing, amazing,' he said later. 'The Cubans will never forget it. Here were people going nuts – for ballet! Everyone I knew wanted tickets – my family, my English teacher, my maths teacher – all who watched me grow.' The once-reluctant, rebellious student returned to his homeland in unbelievable triumph and acclaim.

The two final performances staged at the Karl Marx Theatre were of Sir Kenneth MacMillan's poignant and dramatic ballet *Manon*. Created in 1974 and based on the eighteenth-century romantic novel by Abbé Prévost, it tells the story of a beautiful young girl who falls in love with a penniless young poet, only to turn to prostitution to satisfy her love of money and jewels. It is one of those roles that all ballerinas dream of – Ballet Nacional's prima ballerina Viengsay Valdés said that she would love to be given the opportunity to dance it, that it was at the top of her wish list of roles. In the Cuban premiere, Tamara Rojo took the title role of the young Manon and her poet lover was Carlos. Both have danced the ballet many times before and they always bring a true sense of beauty and drama to their dancing. 'Carlos is an amazing partner,' says Tamara. 'He has a natural instinct but, more important, is very musical so I just can let myself go because I know he will be there every time I need him. He is also very passionate and real good fun to work with.' Their performances are always spectacular but this was a very special evening for the audiences watching them. This was the first MacMillan ballet to be seen live in Cuba and there was great interest by all the Cuban dancers in studying the technicalities of a contemporary classical Western work.

The Royal Ballet's successful visit helped to open the way for New York-based American Ballet Theatre to be invited to perform at the *Festival Internacional de Ballet de la Habana* in November 2010 – its first visit to Cuba in fifty years. Earlier that summer, President Barack Obama had lifted restrictions to open cultural doors between the US and Cuba, though the tourist travel ban still remained.

In April 2010, nine months after The Royal Ballet's visit, it was the turn of the Cubans to return the favour and come to dance in the United Kingdom. Alas there was no blazing sunshine to greet them – indeed it was decidedly chilly so the central heating in the dressing rooms of the London Coliseum was pumped up to a stifling temperature to keep the scantily clad dancers warm for their performances. However, the Cubans seemed happy to be in the British capital, which for many was their first visit there. With just a handful of the older, well-known stars – Viengsay Valdés being one of them – the company this time was mainly made up of new enthusiastic young people who quickly showed that the next generation of Cuban dancers has been well trained. For added excitement, it was announced that Carlos would be dancing four times with them – twice as Prince Siegfried in *Swan Lake* and two performances of the exuberant *Don Quixote pas de deux* in the *Magio de la Danza* divertissement programme. Of course these performances of higher priced tickets sold out as soon as they went on sale, both in London and in the other cities that the company visited. It was while touring with the company that Carlos received the awful news that his mother was very ill. Torn as to where his loyalties lay, he dutifully stayed and fulfilled his obligations to his public and his old company before speeding back to Cuba. But sadly, a flight delay resulted in him arriving just too late to see his mother before she died. It was a bitter blow to lose her.

To many of the British critics, the Cuban productions looked fusty with the choreography oversimplified and often unmusical in Madame Alonso's re-stagings for the very different public taste in Cuba. However, the audiences were wowed by the unison of the corps de ballet in *Swan Lake* and the techniques and zest of the dancers in the mixed programme. In *Swan Lake*, Carlos demonstrated a refined Prince showing off his musicality and subtle classical technique in the white acts. In the third act, he and Viengsay blazed through their riveting *pas de deux*, exuding *joie de vivre* and gay abandonment in her multiple *fouettés* while he, bewitched by her, soared with airborne leaps and furious turns.

'It was one of my best achievements to have taken The Royal Ballet to Cuba,' says Carlos proudly. 'My country is so different to the West, and has so few resources. It meant a lot to my people to see me dancing with my other company and for them to see the kind of new works that I dance. But Ballet Nacional is very dear to me. I am still a member of that company and so was naturally very happy to join them in London. It was exciting for us all.'

CONCLUSION

Finale – But Not the Final Curtain

'I am proud to be a dancer'

IT WAS THE RETIREMENT of The Royal Ballet's ballerina Darcey Bussell that made a huge impression on Carlos. Unlike an actor, singer or musician, the career of a ballet dancer comes to a close far too early in the performing life, just when the techniques have been polished and the emotional input is at its best. For a ballerina, it is usually around forty years of age; for a man it's earlier, if they want to be remembered fondly. Rudolf Nureyev continued dancing classical works into his late forties, far longer than most thought wise – and his last appearance in a character role was at the age of fifty-four when he appeared as the Fairy Carabosse in *The Sleeping Beauty*. His technique had all but disappeared though he could still offer a mesmerising presence on stage. For Carlos, the day draws ever closer and he realistically recognises that the physical demands of classical ballet dancing are for the very young. On 8 June 2007, Darcey performed for the last time with The Royal Ballet, having decided that at the age of thirty-eight years, it was time to leave the stage. It was a huge shock to all her fans and colleagues for she was still in fantastic form physically and technically, and much loved. But that was how she wanted to be remembered and she had made her decision. She chose to dance MacMillan's *Song of the Earth* (music Gustav Mahler: *Das Lied von der Erde*) as her final piece in the gala of her favourite roles. Her performance in this haunting and heart-rending work, in which Carlos danced as the Messenger of Death, marked the end of her stunning career, and at the curtain call, she received a standing ovation lasting over eight minutes. The evening was televised live by the BBC to a greater audience. The gala made thirty-seven-year-old Carlos think of his own career and of how much longer he would be able to dance his roles. 'I can't believe that it was Darcey's last performance,' he said. 'It was so poignant dancing with her. All through it I kept thinking, "This will be me in a few years time." You are only as good as your last show and you are constantly racing against time – the human body is not made for ballet. It's unnatural in the way we have to train to get perfect turn-out, high extensions, strong feet. It takes time to become recognised as a principal. Then suddenly after thirty years of age, you realise that you have reached your peak and will soon have to stop. It's so different to the other arts. A dancer has a short life. One day I shall have to hang up my shoes – and that day draws closer and closer. I want to go while I can still dance – I owe it to my audience and to my own self-respect.'

As that moment draws ever nearer, Carlos has been developing different aspects of his multi-faceted talent, assuring his public that he will not disappear from the spotlight when his tights and ballet shoes have been packed away for the last time.

Following on from his successful *Tocororo*, he has been expanding his producer skills by bringing different dance productions to the London stages during the summer months when resident companies have closed for the season. In these, he dances with colleagues, both from London and from Havana. His crowd-pleasing 'Carlos Acosta and Friends' divertissement evenings have been packed with the expected firecracker technical feats, calm classical moments, exuberant Cuban pizzazz and competitive macho men streaking across, over, around the stage. Yet Carlos has chosen not to rely on the usual fare of classical snippets alone for such programmes – though he has included a token few to show off his and his dancers' fantastic techniques

– and has presented works new to the British public and often with a Cuban or South American flavour. While some of these are not to everyone's taste, he has shown courage in going against offering the expected 'party pieces'. And his vision hasn't harmed box-office receipts.

In July 2010, he produced a completely new view of himself in *Premieres*, a programme which offered only contemporary works, and received a mixed reception. Those who had come to see 'Carlos, the high-flier' were disappointed. While the Cuban still performs with extraordinary muscularity and power, contemporary moves are somewhat new to him, and he has a long way to go before he can compete with the top dancers in this field. He wrote in the programme that this was 'not a feel-good show', and many had to agree. The lighting for *Premieres* was as dark as was the mood throughout, despite using some digital reality effects. Carlos had invited only one other dancer to join him, Zenaida Yanowsky, a principal at The Royal Ballet, renowned for her regal and lyrical classicism. However, the pieces the two dancers performed showed neither of them in the magnificent style normally associated with their artistic skills, and the evening of short solos and few duets was over, even with an interval, in one hour and forty minutes.

Throughout his early years at The Royal Ballet, Carlos was absorbed in writing down his memoirs – 'I didn't read a proper book until I was twenty-five,' he laughingly admits. But he has felt liberated enough to put into words the extraordinary life he has led. In 2007, he published his autobiography, *No Way Home*, (in Spanish it translates as 'Don't Look Back') and the book has sold well. It is a very frank, simply told story in which he bares his soul and speaks honestly of the challenges he has faced during his life. 'Writing my own history down helped to ease the pain of my loneliness,' he admits. In December 2007, a condensation of the book was chosen for BBC Radio 4's *Book of the Week*. Now, after this first literary success, he has embarked on a historic novel about slavery in Cuba – 'I love the research and establishing the characters,' he enthuses.

His personality and good interviewing skills are sought out by the media and he was invited to appear on one of the BBC's oldest and most popular radio programmes, *Desert Island Discs*, where the guest has to imagine being marooned on an island. While telling his life story, he is asked which eight favourite records he wants to take with him. Carlos chose an eclectic array of music from ballet pieces to a particular Cuban favourite bursting with hip-moving rhythms called 'Bacalao con Pan', performed by Irakere. Apparently, according to the interviewer Sue

McGregor, they were both up and out of their chairs, dancing in the recording studio when the piece was played. For the luxury that he was allowed to take, he chose Cuban cigars. Carlos has also been pursued to appear on various television chat shows, has been filmed demonstrating ballet technique in master classes, and he has been the subject of several documentaries. *YouTube* abounds with short sensational snippets of his dancing.

Carlos has been honoured many times in his life, in many countries. In 2003, he received the top prize at the Critics' Circle National Dance Award for Best Male Dancer. In 2007, he picked up the Outstanding Achievement in Dance prize at the Laurence Olivier Awards for *Tocororo;* he won *Dance Europe*'s Readers' Award, and there have been many other honours. The young ruffian from Los Pinos, who constantly played truant at school, today holds the title of Doctor of Letters, an honorary award from London's Metropolitan University. He received the honour in 2006, dressed in a mauve and grey academic gown and soft mauve mortarboard complete with tassel. Fortunately for all, many of his performances have been filmed and the DVDs are sold around the world. So, like a pop star, Carlos has a Decca contract – 'I think I'm the first dancer to do this,' he chuckles.

With his good looks, easy manner and now good

English, it was no wonder that he got a call asking him to appear in a film. It was his friend, the actress Natalie Portman, who had written a role with him in mind into the script of *New York I Love You*, a movie which was released in 2009. In the film, he plays the father of a little girl whom he takes for a walk in Central Park. Because she is blonde, it is assumed that he is her babysitter. It was a cameo role lasting about seven minutes but he enjoyed jetting over to Manhattan to film.

He also appears in *Days of the Flowers* in the role of Tomas, a tourist guide who falls in love on the island of Cuba. He would fly over between commitments to film and found the process very different from his usual way of working. 'When I dance, I go on stage and, from A to Z, we are living the story chronologically. In the film, we had to go and give what was required whenever we were called, even though the scenes were out of synchronisation – and it might not be the best moment for you to dig up the emotion. I soon realised that true cinema filming is "wait, wait, wait". But even so, I'm ready to do more!'

Carlos didn't defect, didn't criticise Castro or the system in Cuba and has remained loyal to his teachers, friends and family. He has become an unofficial cultural ambassador for his country and his art for the past twenty years. Because of his unique relationship with his home country, Carlos is reticent about discussing Cuban politics and keeps his thoughts to himself. 'Of course I have political views but they are irrelevant for others to know,' he says. 'I am not a politician. I'm an artist. I separate art from politics, though obviously the arts cannot survive without politics.'

Despite his humble beginnings and the challenges he has had to face in his lifetime, the name of Carlos Acosta is today known worldwide. His recognised super-bravura technique, his dramatic acting and his natural personable charisma on stage have won him fans all over the globe. 'My trademarks are my technical abilities and the power to jump high,' he says. 'But I also believe that it is because of my unusual background – and maybe the colour of my skin – that have also helped to put me in the spotlight. Remember that the audiences here in London had never seen a black Romeo before me! I try to bring a different range of emotions and characteristics to my roles so that the people can see a believable character and not "Carlos in another costume".' Throughout his life, he has remained loyal to his mentor and teacher Ramona de Saá (Chery) and she to him. 'We have a history together,' she says. 'Professionally he had to be out of my hands, but I am so proud of him, about everything that he has accomplished. And he is still the same person we wanted him to be. Now he is a man of responsibility.'

During his dancing career, Carlos has helped to put Cuba on the world's cultural map, showing his homeland in a favourable light, thus deserving the adulation and loyal dedication that his countrymen give him. His life experiences have richly coloured his stage performances and, despite his reluctant beginnings, the specific characteristics and exuberance for dance that he learned through hardship to love, together with his incredible natural talent, have touched the hearts of thousands. 'Ballet saved me and it shaped me, and I shall always be grateful to my father for that. I'm grateful too to have had so many opportunities in my career. Working abroad has taught me much and I have grown as a dancer. I shall always be a product of the Ballet Nacional de Cuba despite my connections with many different companies. Living so many years abroad, I question the price that I have had to pay for my fame. As with everything in life, you have to lose something in order to gain something else. For me, it was leaving my family, my country, my culture and my language, to work abroad. I missed out on home life by always living out of suitcases, and I still do. But I try to take my Cuban identity with me everywhere I go. It's all very well meeting royalty and famous people but inside me, I'd rather be home in Havana playing dominoes and drinking rum with my family and friends. I now have my own home there so I have somewhere to come when I finish classical dancing,' wistfully adding, 'and I would like to have a family of my own.' He has mentioned the possibilities of starting a new company based in Cuba, would like to dance modern works, to act in films and even sing in musicals if the opportunities arise. 'I'm very creative and need to use my brain in finding different ways to express myself,' he says. He certainly has no intention of disappearing from view when he retires from the classical ballet stage.

'Changes will come to Cuba in the future – hopefully not too great or shocking. I don't want to see McDonald's and Starbucks on every corner. Cuba must retain the soul of its people – that's what makes my country so special. I am proud to be a Cuban. And I am proud to be a dancer.'

Biography

2 June 1973	Carlos Junior Acosta Quesada born in Los Pinos, Havana, Cuba.
1982	Starts at the Alejo Carpentier Provincial School of Ballet.
1985	Expelled and enrols at the Vocational Arts School, Pinar del Río.
1987	Returns to Havana and is accepted into the National School of the Arts – the National School of Ballet.
1989	Penultimate year of training spent in the company of Teatro Nuevo, Turin, Italy.
1990	Awarded the Gold Medal at the Prix de Lausanne, Switzerland. Awarded the Grand Prix at the Paris International Dance Competition, France.

Graduates with highest mark and gold medal from Cuba's National School of Ballet; is offered a place in the corps de ballet of the Ballet Nacional de Cuba but goes to London as principal with English National Ballet.

1992	Returns to Cuba for an operation and doesn't dance for nearly a year. Given the position of soloist with Ballet Nacional de Cuba.
1993	Becomes a principal of Houston Ballet, Texas, USA.
1998	Joins The Royal Ballet, London as its first black principal.
2003	Creates and stages his first ballet *Tocororo – A Cuban Tale*, in Havana and London.
2007	Invited to dance *Spartacus* with the Bolshoi Ballet in Moscow.
2009	Returns to Cuba to perform with The Royal Ballet Company.
2010	Dances with the Ballet Nacional de Cuba in London.

Acknowledgements

Carlos: I am sincerely grateful for your patience, intelligence, respect, wit and kindness over the two decades that I have known and interviewed you. I had not realised until I started setting down on paper, how many fascinating details I had stored in my mind since our first meeting, and it's been a joy to have spent so much time thinking about you during these past months.

My heartfelt thanks go to so many people worldwide who have given their precious time to discuss all things 'Carlos' with me. These are:

London: At The Royal Ballet: Dame Monica Mason, artistic director ('I love to talk about Carlos'): Tamara Rojo, principal ballerina; David Makhateli, principal dancer, and Rosie Neave and Kitty Greenleaf in the Press Office, who organised for me to go through the company's archival material.

Rachel Branton, Press Manager at English National Ballet for answering my queries about Carlos' time with that company. Andy Wood, director of ¡Como No! and Alistair Spalding, chief executive and artistic director of Sadler's Wells Theatre who gave me insights into their work presenting Carlos to new audiences on different stages and in diverse works.

Russia: From the Bolshoi Ballet, Moscow: Boris Akimov, former artistic director, principal dancer, teacher and coach; Ludmila Semenyaka, former principal ballerina, now coach; Mikhail Lavrovsky, former principal dancer, now coach, Nina Kaptsova, leading soloist.

From the Mikhailovsky Ballet, St Petersburg: Mikhail Messerer, Ballet master-in-chief, and respected international teacher.

The Republic of Georgia: Nina Ananiashvili, former prima ballerina of the Bolshoi Ballet, now artistic director and prima ballerina of the Georgian State Ballet.

America: From Houston Ballet: Ben Stevenson OBE, former artistic director, now artistic director of Texas Ballet Theater, for his keen and humorous comments: Lauren Anderson, former prima ballerina; plus the stalwart research work by the head of press, Andrew

Edmondson, now Director of Marketing and Public Relations, who delved deeply into archives to give me the much appreciated facts and details I needed.

Paris: Reunion with dear friends, Olga Guardia Smoak and Janet O'Keeffe who share my love of Carlos, and who contributed new facets of his life.

And of course:

Cuba: Where my gratitude goes first to Madame Alicia Alonso, founder of the Ballet Nacional de Cuba, for her elegant lunchtime chats; to Fernando Alonso for his conversation about the National School of Ballet, to Loipa Araujo, ex ballerina, now teacher and coach, Viengsay Valdés, prima ballerina of Ballet Nacional de Cuba, and to Carlos' great mentor and surrogate mother, Ramona de Saá, the director of the National School of Ballet, a truly remarkable woman who gave me insights into her experiences with young Carlos.

And then there is my interpreter and dear friend in Havana, Mareylis Lorenzo Molina, who has constantly been on the lookout for any scrap of Cuban news about Carlos to e-mail me. But my greatest thanks must go to Ismael S. Albelo, professor and dance critic who has been my lifeline, answering by return, and in red ink, the many, many e-mailed questions that flew through the airways, and for keeping me up to date with every detail of the Cuban ballet scene. I certainly couldn't have done the book without him. Muchas gracías, Albelo.

Back in London again, my thanks go to Rosemarie Hudson, editor of the BlackAmber Inspirations series who initially invited me to write the book, and to Angeline Rothermundt at Arcadia Books who put all my musings together. And I also offer much gratitude to the photographers whose wonderful pictures adorn this book – Angela Taylor, Robbie Jack and John Ross.

And finally, my love and thanks to my family: to my three children who, though scattered on different continents of the world, regularly e-mailed and phoned with encouragement. And, like Carlos, I am most grateful for the loving support and understanding of my own mother.
Thank you everyone.

Esher, Surrey 2010